D1565954

ISBN 978-0-282-03922-6
PIBN 10128501

1 MONTH OF FREE READING

at

www.ForgottenBooks.com

By purchasing this book you are eligible for one month membership to ForgottenBooks.com, giving you unlimited access to our entire collection of over 1,000,000 titles via our web site and mobile apps.

To claim your free month visit:

www.forgottenbooks.com/free128501

English
Français
Deutsche
Italiano
Español
Português

www.forgottenbooks.com

Mythology Photography **Fiction**
Fishing Christianity **Art** Cooking
Essays Buddhism Freemasonry
Medicine **Biology** Music **Ancient**
Egypt Evolution Carpentry Physics
Dance Geology **Mathematics** Fitness
Shakespeare **Folklore** Yoga Marketing
Confidence Immortality Biographies
Poetry **Psychology** Witchcraft
Electronics Chemistry History **Law**
Accounting **Philosophy** Anthropology
Alchemy Drama Quantum Mechanics
Atheism Sexual Health **Ancient History**
Entrepreneurship Languages Sport
Paleontology Needlework Islam
Metaphysics Investment Archaeology
Parenting Statistics Criminology
Motivational

THREE PAPERS.

Read before the Chicago Historical Society:

KASKASKIA AND ITS PARISH RECORDS.
OLD FORT CHARTRES.
COL. JOHN TODD'S RECOR

By EDWARD G. MASON.

imes; Embracing also The History of My Life. By JOHN REYNOLDS, Late
., etc. Portrait. Reprint of original edition of 1855, with complete Index added. Cloth boards;
ide and bottom uncut; Antique Paper; Pp 425; 8vo. 1879. Edition of 112 copies. Price, $7.50.

ased to learn that the Fergus Print-
y has undertaken the work of re-
volume of "My Own Times: embrac-
History of My Life," written by the
n Reynolds. * * * Copies of
eferred to are exceedingly rare, and
be procured at any price. The
re
so
a
epi
a
wh
a
n
y
om
o
t
ld
m
t r
in
in
sor
de
ot
w
abl
int
l e
olu
It
et
o a
ul
is
v w
m
807
po
wi
d
its
he
e
re
tt
e,
r
ask
e, a
t, W
ve
ttle
atic
of
rob
e time when the parents of Gov.
lds removed to Illinois from Ten-
added the seventh family to the
f a white settlement two and a-half
skaskia. Gov. Reynolds was then
In the volume before us he de-
ondition of the country, the Ind-
ations of the whites, their progress
e, education, government and so-
ristics during the next nine years,
ble length, and thus furnishes a
l and interesting information.

About this time, having reached his 20th year,
the Governor entered a college some six miles
from Knoxville, Tenn., where he spent two years
in improving his mind, returning to Illinois in
1811. Afterward he studied law at Knoxville.

Then began the War of 1812 with Great Britain, and then, too, the growing State of Illinois
of stirring public events
inent place in the history
apters are devoted to this
massacre at Chicago, the
and affairs in that vicini-

nization of the Territory
stration of Governor Ed-
the laws, and the first
d Clark's expedition to
extension of the settle-
egulators" and mob-law;
s denominations in Illi-
the history of slavery in
author's domestic record,
events of more or less in-

rnment was formed, and
detail. A large space is
nt political history and
of the State, until the
ar with the Winnebago
pters are filled with the
vk war and its attendant
. The history of educa-
pers in Illinois receives

lates the national situa-
n Congress from 1834 to
t to Europe in 1839; the
tions in the State; the
nois - and - Michigan Ca-
nal improvements, and
non troubles and excite-

of Gov. Reynolds' book.
ng the spirit of the pio-
and as the record of a
State struggling against
and becoming one of the
aerican commonwealths.
story of Gov. Reynolds,
ecutive and Representa-
interest the reader. He
use he aided in bringing
perity which she enjoys.
a century in prominent
s Judge Advocate, Judge
member of the Legisla-
ssman, Canal Commis-
the House—and is so
closely Identified with the State that their his-
tories can not be separated.

This volume was first published by Gov. Reynolds in 1855. The edition was small, and most
of it was destroyed before it was sold in a fire in
Chicago. Thus it became one of the lost books
of the earth. Fortunately it was not totally exterminated, and now its revival by the enter-
prising Chicago house whose imprint it bears is
no less important than it is gratifying to those
who have the interests of the State at heart.—
Chicago Journal, Dec. 30, 1879.

ent by mail, post-paid, on receipt of price.

ILLINOIS IN THE EIGHTEENTH CENTURY.

KASKASKIA AND ITS PARISH RECORDS:

OLD FORT CHARTRES:

AND

COL. JOHN TODD'S RECORD-BOOK:

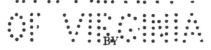

BY

EDWARD G. MASON,

CHICAGO.

CHICAGO:

FERGUS PRINTING COMPANY.

1881.

KASKASKIA AND ITS PARISH RECORDS.

A Paper read before the Chicago Historical Society, Dec. 16, 1879.

IN Southern Illinois, near the Mississippi, a hundred miles or more above the mouth of the Ohio, is situated the ancient village of Kaskaskia, supposed to be the oldest permanent European settlement in the valley of the Father of the waters. The eminent historian who concedes to it this distinction finds it difficult to fix the date of its origin, and leaves that undetermined.* Its foundation has been variously ascribed to members of La Salle's expedition to the mouth of the Mississippi on their return in 1682,† to Father James Gravier in 1683 or in 1685,‡ to Tonti in 1686,§ and to. others still, missionaries or explorers, at different dates in the latter part of the seventeenth century. But the uncertainty upon this point has arisen, in part at least, from the confounding of Kaskaskia with an earlier Indian settlement of the same name on the Illinois River, where was established the Jesuit mission afterwards removed to the existing village. And this, perhaps, will be more apparent from a brief sketch of the history of that mission.

When Father Marquette returned from his adventurous voyage upon the Mississippi in 1673, by the way of the Illinois, he found on the latter river a village of the Illinois tribe, containing seventy-four cabins, which was called Kaskaskia. Its inhabitants received him well, and obtained from him a promise to return and instruct them. He kept that promise faithfully, undaunted by disease and toilsome journeys and inclement weather, and, after a rude wintering by the Chicago River, reached the Illinois village again, April 8th, 1675.‖ The site of this Indian settlement has since been identified with the great meadow south of the modern Town of Utica in the State of Illinois, and nearly opposite to the tall cliff soon after known as Fort St. Louis of the Illinois, and in later times as Starved Rock.¶ Marquette

---

* Bancroft's History of the United States, I. p. 195.
† Davidson and Stuve's History of Illinois, p. 110.
‡ Atlas of State of Illinois, pp. 169, 202.
§ Montague's History of Randolph County, Illinois, p. 12.
‖ Shea's Discovery and Exploration of the Mississippi, p. 55.
¶ Parkman's Discovery of the Great West, p. 69.

established there a mission, to which he gave the name of the Immaculate Conception of the Blessed Virgin, and, for a little time, was able to teach the chiefs and the people. But continued illness soon obliged him to set forth upon that return voyage which brought him to a lonely grave in the wilderness.

To him succeeded the zealous priest, Claude Allouez, who seems to have been at the mission the following year, and at all events reached it in April, 1677. He was lodged, as he says, in Marquette's cabin, and erected a cross 25 feet high in the midst of the town, which the old men earnestly commended him to place well so that it could not fall. Departing shortly after, he returned in 1678, but the incursions of the resistless warriors of the Five Nations scattered the Illinois, and checked the mission, and the approach of La Salle, who was unfriendly to him, compelled Allouez's retirement the following year. The attempts of the priests who accompanied La Salle to continue the work, were set at naught by the attacks of the Iroquois upon the Illinois, who fled before their fierce oppressors. In 1684, however, Allouez returned under more favorable auspices, and was at the mission the greater part of the time until his death in 1690.

He was followed by the famous Jesuit, Sabastian Rasle, who embarked in a canoe at Quebec, in August, 1691, to go to the Illinois, and completed his journey of more than eight hundred leagues the following spring. Within two years, he was recalled to his original charge among the Abnaki Indians, to find a martyr's fate long after at the hands of New England soldiers by the waters of the Kennebec.

Father James Gravier, who had been at the mission during Allouez's absence in 1687, received it from Father Rasle, and built a chapel within the walls of Fort St. Louis which overlooked the village. His journal of the Mission of the Immaculate Conception of Our Lady at the Illinois from March 20th, 1693, to February 15th, 1694, gives a very interesting account of his labors among the Indians upon the Illinois River.* This, it will be noticed, is ten years or more after the time when some have supposed he founded the present Kaskaskia, three hundred miles or more to the southward, upon the Mississippi. The Illinois nation or confederacy was composed of five bands or tribes, the Kaskaskias, the Peorias, the Cahokias, the Tamaroas, and the Mitchigamias. Gravier's work was principally among the first of these, but extended also to the Peorias. He longed to include in it the Tamaroas and the Cahokias, who were on the Mississippi, between his mission and the site of the Kaskaskia of

* Shea's History of Catholic Missions, pp. 410–415.

to-day, but was unable to do more than to make them a single
brief visit, because he was alone in the land. Of the Mitchigamias, who were still lower down the great river, but north of
the place he is said to have founded in 1683 or 1685, and whose
village he must have passed in order to reach it, Gravier seems
hardly to have heard, and it is but reasonable to infer that at the
date of his journal he had not traveled as far as their settlement.

During his stay in this region, Father Gravier studied the
language of the Illinois, and reduced it to grammatical rules, and
was regarded by his successors as the real founder of the mission,
because he ensured its permanency.* When recalled to Michilimackinac, about 1699, he left the Fathers Bineteau and Pinet
in charge of the different branches of the original establishment,
and with them labored Gabriel Marest, who seems to have been
particularly associated with the Kaskaskia tribe. It will readily
be seen that in the writings of such a number of missionaries, at
these various dates, concerning a mission frequently spoken of as
at Kaskaskia, or the village of the Kaskaskias, many allusions might
occur which would seem to refer to the present place of the name.

But the evidence that this mission remained upon the Illinois
River until the year 1700, and that there was no settlement before
that time upon the site of the Kaskaskia we now know, appears
to be well-nigh conclusive. A letter written to the Bishop of
Quebec by John Francis Buisson de St. Cosme, a missionary
priest, describes the journey of his party from Michilimackinac
to the mouth of the Arkansas, by the Illinois and Mississippi
Rivers, in the year 1699.† They stayed at the house of the
Jesuit Fathers at Chicago, and set out from there about November first, on what one of their predecessors calls the divine river,
named by the Indians Checagou, and made the portage to the
River of the Illinois. Passing the Illinois village before referred
to, they learned that most of the Indians had gone to Peoria
Lake to hunt. Arriving there, they met the Fathers Pinet and
Maret, with their flock, of which St. Cosme gives a good account,
and he speaks of their work as the Illinois mission. The party
journeyed onward, under the guidance of La Salle's trusty
lieutenant, Tonti. While on the Illinois River, certain Indians
attempted to prevent their going to the Mississippi, and intimated
that they would be killed if they did so. Tonti replied that he
did not fear men, that they had seen him meet the Iroquois, and
knew that he could kill men; and the Indians offered no further
opposition. They reached the Mississippi the 6th of December,

* Marest's Letter, Kip. p. 206.
† Early Voyages up and down the Mississippi, p. 43.

1699, and the next day reached the village of the Tamaroas, who had never seen any "black gown," except for a few days when the reverend Father Gravier paid them a visit. A week later, they ascended a rock on the right, going down the river, and erected a beautiful cross, which their escort saluted with a volley of musketry, and St. Cosme prayed that God might grant that the cross, which had never been known in those regions, might triumph there. From the context of the letter, it is evident that this ceremony took place not far below the site of the present Kaskaskia, which St. Cosme must have passed to reach this rock, but he makes no mention of such a village. Furthermore, within fifteen miles or so of Kaskaskia, there is a rocky bluff on the Missouri side of the river, known now as the Cape of the Five Men, or Cap Cinq Hommes. This doubtless is a corruption of the name of the good Father St. Cosme, as appears from a map made a little more than one hundred years ago, which gives both names, Cinqhommes and St. Cosme, to this very bluff. It probably is the identical one which he ascended, and he could not have spoken of the cross as unknown in those regions, had there been any settlement so near the spot as the Kaskaskia we now know. Tonti, who was the leader of this party, is thought by some to have founded Kaskaskia in 1686. Nobler founder could no town have had than this faithful and fearless soldier, but the facts just narrated make such a theory impossible.

Again, in the early part of the year 1700, a bold voyager, Le Sueur, whose journal is in print,* pushed up the Mississippi from its mouth, where D'Iberville had just planted the banner of France, and passed the site of Kaskaskia, without notice of such a place. He speaks of the village of the Tamaroas, where, by this time, St. Cosme had taken up his abode on his return from the south. About July 15th, going northward, Le Sueur arrived at the mouth of the Illinois, and there met three Canadian *voyageurs* coming to join his party, and received by them a letter from the Jesuit Marest, dated July 10th, 1700, at the Mission of the Immaculate Conception of the Blessed Virgin at the Illinois. The letter of St. Cosme, and the journal of Le Sueur, seem to show clearly enough that down to the middle of the year 1700, the present Kaskaskia had not been settled, and that the Mission was still on the Illinois River.

And lastly, we have the journal of the voyage of Father James Gravier, in 1700, from the country of the Illinois to the mouth of the Mississippi;† from which we learn that he returned from Michilimackinac, and set out from Chicago on the 8th of Sep-

---

* Early Voyages up and down the Mississippi, p. 92.   † P. 116.

tember, 1700. He says he arrived too late at the Illinois, of whom Father Marest had charge, to prveent the transmigration of the village of the Kaskaskias, which was too precipitately made, on vague news of the establishment on the Mississippi, evidently referring to the landing of D'Iberville the year before. He did not believe that the Kaskaskias, whom Marest accompanied, would have separated from the Peorias and other Illinois, had he arrived sooner; and he obtained a promise from the Peorias to await his return from the Mississippi. After having marched four days with the Kaskaskias, Gravier went forward with Marest, whom he left sick at the Tamaroas village, and departed from there October 9th, 1700, to go to the lower part of the Mississippi, accompanied only by some Frenchmen. The Indians with Marest, we may presume, halted upon the peninsula between the Kaskaskia and the Mississippi Rivers, where we soon after find them; and thus doubtless was accomplished the transfer of the mission to its final location. The eagerness of the Illinois tribes to be in closer communication with the French was probably intensified by their desire to escape any further assaults from their dreaded enemies, and to rear their wigwams where they would never hear the war-cry of the Iroquois. Both motives would operate more powerfully with the Kaskaskias than with any others, because they had been longer under the influence of the French, and because, in their old location, they were the first to receive the onslaughts of the relentless foemen of the Illinois. Hence they set out to go to the lower Mississippi, but Gravier's influence, and perhaps Marest's illness as well, led them to pause at the first suitable resting-place, and that became their permanent abode. And when we consider that a few years later, this same Father Marest, who accompanied these Indians on their migration, was stationed at the present Kaskaskia, in charge of the Mission of the Immaculate Conception, as appears from his letters;* that he died and was buried there, as is shown by the parish records;† and that we hear nothing further of a mission of this name on the Illinois River; we may reasonably conclude that the Kaskaskia of our time should date its origin from the fall of of the year 1700, and should honor James Gravier and Gabriel Marest as its founders.

From Marest's letters we know that some Frenchmen inter-married with the Indians of this village, and dwelt there, and we may naturally infer that their presence attracted others of their race, trappers, fur traders, and *voyageurs* to the new location. And so, almost at the dawn of the history of the territory included

* Marest's Letter, Kip. p. 197.
† Kaskaskia Parish Records, p. 9. Burial Register.

within the limits of the State of Illinois, the present Kaskaskia was inhabited by a mixed population of whites and Indians, under the sway of the priest of the Order of Jesus. At first a mission simply, then a trading station, and soon a military post; within twenty years from its foundation, it had enough of the features of a permanent settlement to justify the worthy priests in organizing there a parish, which succeeded to their beloved mission, and was known by the same name.

A large portion of the church .records of this parish, beginning perhaps with its establishment, and some extracts from those of the earlier mission, have fortunately been preserved to this day; and they throw many a curious and interesting side-light upon the events of the times in which they were written. Of their authenticity there can be no question. Some of them are still in the custody of the priest of the parish, and others are in the possession of a prelate* of the church that has labored so long and so zealously in the region of which these records illustrate the history. By his thoughtful care, the earlier books, which suffered damage at Kaskaskia in the flood of 1844, were removed to a place of greater security. And recently the volumes containing the entries made between the years 1695 and 1835 have been arranged and re-bound, and with proper care may remain a monument of the early history of what is now the State of Illinois for many years to come.

In the re-binding, has been preserved intact the old parchment cover of the first of these records, on which may be dimly traced in the faded ink the words *"Registrum pro anno 1696,"* but the remainder of the inscription is too indistinct to be deciphered. Probably it is the same in which Father Marest carried the scanty records of the mission at its removal. The originals of these mission records have not been preserved, and we have in their stead a copy of a portion only, entitled *"Extrait des Regitres de Bapteme de la Mission des Illinois sous le titre de l'Immaculeé Conseption de la S. V."* The copy itself, a small quarto of six pages, is in Latin, and the first entry is of the baptism, March 20th, 1695, by James Gravier, of Pierre Aco, the newly born son of Michael Aco and Maria Aramipinchicoue. The godfather was D. de Mautchy, in whose place stood D. Montmidy, and the godmother was Maria Joanna, grandmother of the boy. This Michael Aco was one of the Frenchmen who accompanied Father Hennepin on his journey to the Upper Mississippi, when the Falls of St. Anthony were discovered and named, and probably was the leader of the party, although the intrepid falsifier, Hennepin,

---

* Right Reverend P. J. Baltes, Bishop of Alton, Ill.

assumes that honor for himself in his account of the expedition. Aco's wife was the daughter of the chief of the Kaskaskias, and Gravier's journal describes their marriage in 1693. She was a convert, and through her influence her parents embraced Christianity, and she rendered great service to the missionaries as a teacher of the children. The boy, Pierre Aco, lived to be a citizen of the second Kaskaskia, and the transcript of the old French title records now in the office of the recorder of Randolph County, Illinois, contains a deed from him of a lot in Kaskaskia, executed September 12th, 1725. The two other entries in the mission record in 1695 are of the baptisms of children of French fathers and Indian mothers; the second of Michael, son of Jean Colon La Violette and Catherine Ekipakinoua, whose godfather was Michael Aco. It is curious to notice the difficulty the good fathers seem to have found in writing the names of the Indian women who appeared at these baptisms, as mothers and godmothers of the infants, as shown by their use of Greek characters for this purpose. We can imagine them standing at the font, listening to the many syllabled titles of parents and sponsors, smoothly uttered in the Illinois tongue, and vainly trying to reproduce them, until in despair they have resource to their classical learning for symbols of something akin to the new sounds.

In the year 1697, another son of La Violette and Catherine of the lengthy name, was baptized by Father Julian Bineteau, who had been a missionary in Maine in 1693, and the next year was stationed on the St. Lawrence. St. Cosme met him at Chicago, in 1699, when he had recently come in from the Illinois and was ill. He died, not long after, while following his Indians on their summer hunt over the parched prairies, when fatigue and exposure led to a severe sickness, of which he expired in the arms of his devoted colleague, Gabriel Marest.

In September, 1699, Father Marest baptized Theresa Panicoue; and the same year, in November, another son of La Violette was baptized by De Montigny of the same party with St. Cosme, and Tonti was the godfather. St. Cosme in the letter from which quotation has been made, speaking of their descent of the Illinois and landing at an Indian village, November 28, 1699, says: "We said mass in the cabin of a soldier named La Violette, married to a squaw, whose child Mr. De Montigny baptized." The entry in the mission record and the letter therefore confirm each other.

The first ceremony recorded after the removal of the mission to the present village, is a baptism performed April 17, 1701, by Gabriel Marest; and the first, and indeed the only one at which Gravier officiated, after this removal, occurred April 13, 1703, when he baptized the infant son of Pierre Bizaillon and Maria

Theresia.   No further mention is made of Father Gravier in these records; but we know from other sources that he returned to the Peorias to labor among them, was dangerously wounded in a tumult excited by the medicine men, and descended the river in search of medical treatment, and that his injuries, aggravated by the long voyage, proved fatal to him at Mobile in 1706.

Under date of April 13, 1703, there appears in the midst of the entries of baptisms the single sentence "*Ad ripam Metchagamia dictam venimus.*"   Whether this commemorates an expedition by some priest to the shore of Lake Michigan, which perhaps he gazed upon from the site of Chicago, or a visit to the little river flowing into the Mississippi, by which dwelt the Mitchagamias, who gave their name to both lake and river, we cannot tell.   But it indicates an event which to some one seemed of importance enough to be recorded in the archives of the mission as carefully as were the ceremonies of the church.   In 1707, first appears the name of the Father P. J. Mermet, who came from the great village of the Peorias, after the death of Pinet and Bineteau, to join Marest, with whom he was happily associated for many years. The latter, writing of their life at Kaskaskia, says: "Mermet remains at the village for the instruction of the Indians who stay there, the delicacy of his constitution placing it entirely out of his power to sustain the fatigues of the long journeys.   Nevertheless, in spite of his feeble health, I can say that he is the soul of this mission.   For myself, who am so constituted that I can run on the snow with the rapidity with which a paddle is worked in a canoe, and who have, thanks to God, the strength necessary to endure all these toils, I roam through the forests with the rest of our Indians, much the greater part of whom pass a portion of the winter in the chase."

April 26, 1707, Mermet performs the baptismal ceremony for the daughter of Tiniœ Outauticoue, (godmother Maria Oucanicoue), and George Thorel, commonly called *the Parisian*.   It is strange to think that there should have been at that early day in the western wilderness, one so having so much of the airs and graces of the gay capital of France, as to be known distinctively as its citizen.   The subsequent baptisms at the mission seem all to have been by Mermet and Marest, and the names of the women are usually Indian, including such remarkable ones as Martha Merounouetamoucoue and Domitilla Tehuigouanakigaboucoue.   Occasionally, however, both parents are French. Thus, March 3d, 1715, was baptized Joannes son of Jean Baptiste Potier and Francoise Le Brise, who officiated as godmother at a ceremony in November of the same year.   These are the earliest appearances of one of the matrons of the hamlet,.

who seems from subsequent notices to have afterwards become a perennial godmother. She figures in that capacity on two occasions in 1717, having also presented a child of her own for baptism in that year, and on one of the only two chronicled in 1718, and we find her at the font again in 1719. With an entry made October 2d of the latter year, the baptismal register of the mission proper seems to end; although a very few entries in 1732-3 and 1735 are appended, but these seem to belong rather to the parish.

For the parish, by this time, had been established; and the next in order of these documents is a quarto of twenty-two pages, written in French, as all the rest of these records are, beginning with the *"Registre Des Baptemes faits dans L'eglise de la Mission et dans la Paroisse de la Conception de Ne dame. Commencé le 18 Juin, 1719."* It is evident from this that the mission chapel was still in use, but that a parish had been duly formed. And we learn from the first entry that another element had been added to the population, and that the soldiers of France were at the little village. This is of a baptism performed June 18, 1719, by Le Boullenger of the Society of Jesus, chaplain of the troops, and the godfather is Le Sieur Jacques Bouchart de Verasae, ensign of the troops. We may mention in passing that the infant is the daughter of the marriage of Jean B. Potier and Francoise Le Brise. The priest here named, Joseph Ignatius le Boullenger, is said to have been a man of great missionary tact and wonderful skill in languages. His Illinois catechism, and instructions in the same dialect concerning the mass and the sacraments, were considered to be masterpieces by other missionaries, for whose benefit he prepared a literal French translation. The names of French officers, Charles Legardeur de L'Isle and Claude Charles du Tisné, appear as godfathers in two succeeding entries, and our good friend Francoise Le Brise officiates on both occasions as godmother. We regret to notice that the godmothers as a rule, and she is no exception, declare that they are unable to write, and therefore make their marks. One baptism is of the daughter of a slave woman bearing an Indian name. January 20, 1720, was baptized the son of Charles Danis, a name well known at Kaskaskia as that of one of the first settlers, to whom was made the earliest recorded land-grant in that locality. It was dated May 10, 1722, and executed by Pierre Duque Boisbriant, Knight of the military order of St. Louis, and first king's lieutenant of the province of Louisiana, commanding at the Illinois, and Marc Antoine de la loire des Ursins, principal secretary for the Royal India Company. The godfather for Danis' child was this same Pierre Duque Boisbriant, who was the first military commander in that region, and in one sense may be called the first governor of Illinois.   And about this time we meet with the name of Jean Charles Guymonneau of the Company of Jesus, who was the principal officer of the church at the Illinois, and had special charge of an Indian village six miles inland from the Mississippi.

And now another change takes place, and Kaskaskia is no longer in the pastoral care of a missionary or military chaplain, but has its regular parish priest.   Father Nicholas Ignatius de Beaubois, who describes himself as *"curé de cette Paroisse,"* signalizes his accession by opening a new *"Registre des Baptemes faits dans l'eglise Paroissiale de la Conception de Ne Dame des Cascaskias,"* which he commences July 9, 1720.   And this, perhaps, indicates the time of the substitution of a parish church for the earlier mission chapel.   The entries preceding this date, made by Boullenger and Guymonneau are, as the manuscript plainly shows, copies, and not the original record, and how this happened we speedly learn.   For the precise Beaubois inserts in his register the following statement: "All that which preceeds is an extract which I, Nicholas Ig. de Beaubois, S. J., Curé of the parish of the Conception of our lady of the Cascaskias, certified to be correct and conformed to the original, which I have suppressed because it was not in order, and because it was kept on scattered leaves, and the present extract is signed by two witnesses, who have compared the present copy with the original; the 25th of July, 1720: De Beaubois, S. J."   We could wish that this choleric priest had been a little more patent, or his predecessor a little more careful, for the scattered leaves of that suppressed original contained probably the only autograph of Commandant Boisbriant ever written in the parish register, and would have been a little earlier original record than any we know of now in Illinois. But it was not so to be, and we must content ourselves with the fact that this register which Beaubois began is an undoubted original, containing perhaps the earliest existing manuscript penned in what is now the State of Illinois.   And its opening entry of July 9th, 1720, has a special interest of its own, for the godfather at that baptism was "Le Sieur Pierre D'Artaguiette," captain of a company, and his signature is appended.   He was a gallant young officer of good family in France, who some years later distinguished himself greatly in the wars with the Natchez Indians, and won promotion thereby, and the position of Commandant at the Illinois.   From his station there, in 1736, he marched against the Chickasaws, under the orders of the royal governor of Louisiana, and bravely met a tragic death in the campaign.   Next we have an entry of a child baptized by a soldier, because it was in danger of death before it could be brought to a priest, but Beaubois, nevertheless, performs the ceremony over again. In the year 1720, le Sieur Girardot, ensign of the troops, appears as godfather, and from this time on regularly officiates in that capacity, vieing with Francoise Le Brise in frequency of attendance at the baptismal rite in the character of sponsor. His name was long known in Kaskaskia and its neighborhood, where he spent many years, and it is probably borne to-day by the town of Cape Girardeau in Missouri. In 1721, Le Sieur Nicholas Michel Chassin, Commissary of the Company of the West in the country of the Illinois, signs the register. He was one of the representatives of John Law's famous Mississippi Company, or Company of the West, afterwards merged in the Company of the Indies. In the same year, a child was re-baptized, over whom the ceremony had been once performed, on account of the risk and danger of the voyage up the Mississippi, by le Sieur Noyent, Major de la Place, at New Orleans, September 10, 1720, which seems to show that the date of 1723, usually given for the founding of New Orleans, is incorrect. So too a child, born at the Natchez in December, 1720, and baptized there by a *voyageur*, Pierre La Violette, probably a son of the soldier named in the mission records, was again baptized at Kaskaskia in May, 1721. And in the following June, that worthy woman, Françoise Le Brise, comes once more to the front in her favorite rôle of godmother, and unhesitatingly asserts that she is not able to sign her name, and is permitted to make her mark, which she does with a vigor and emphasis, which indicates that she was a woman of weight and influence in the community. By this time she has a competitor in one Catharine Juillet, who almost divides the honors with her, and who about this period officiates at the baptism of the son of a Pawnee slave, in company with le Sieur Philippe de la Renaudière, *directeur des mines pour la Compagnie d'Occident*, who signs his name to the register. And the succeeding entry is that of the baptism of the son born of the marriage of this Renaudière, who was a great man in the new colony, and the lady Perrine Pivet. This affair was one of state, and to the record of it are affixed the signatures, not only of the parents and the godfather, Le Gardeur de L'Isle, but of D'Artaguiette, Chassin, St. Jean Tonty—perhaps a relative of the great Tonti—Jean Baptiste Girardot and others. The last entry of a baptism in this book is on July 28th, 1721, and no baptismal register between that date and the year 1759 can now be found.

But next in order of time comes the *Registre des Decedes dans la Paroisse de la Conception de Notre Dame des Cascaskias, Commencé le 4e de Janvier 1721*, which begins with "the death in the parish on that day, at two hours after midnight, of Adrien

Robillard, aged about forty-one years, an inhabitant of the parish, married the preceding night to Domitilla Sacatchioucoua. He had made confession and received the viaticum and the sacrament of extreme unction. His body was buried with the accustomed ceremonies in the cemetery of the parish, upon the high ground near the church, the same day of the month and year aforesaid. In witness whereof I have signed. N. Ig. de Beaubois, S. j." In 1721, appears the death of the wife of Francois Freiul, called the Good-Hearted One, of the King's Brigade of Miners; and also a solemn service for the repose of the soul of the deceased Sieur Louis Tessier, church-warden of the said parish, who died at Natchez the third of the month of June. In 1722, an entry is made, which strikingly illustrates the perils which beset the people of that little village on the great river, which was their only means of communication with the nearest settlements, hundreds of miles away. It reads as follows: "The news has come here this day of the death of Alexis Blaye and Laurent Bransart, who were slain upon the Mississippi by the Chickasaws. The day of their death is not known." Then, in a different ink, as if written at another time, is added below: "It was the 5th or 6th of March, 1722." And this state of things is sadly emphasized by the entry immediately following. "The same year, on the 22d of June, was celebrated in the parish church of the Kaskaskias a solemn service for the repose of the soul of the lady Michelle Chauvin, wife of Jacques Nepven, merchant of Montreal, aged about 45 years, and of Jean Michelle Nepven, aged twenty years, and Elizabeth Nepven, aged 13 years, and Susanne Nepven, 8 years, her children. They were slain by the savages from 5 to 7 leagues from the Wabash. It is believed that Jaques Nepven was taken prisoner, and carried away with one young boy, aged about nine years, named Prever, and one young slave girl, not baptized." This family, doubtless, was removing from Canada to Kaskaskia, as a number did about this time, and had traveled the long and weary way by the St. Lawrence and Lakes Ontario and Erie, the Miami River, the portage to the Wabash, and the Ohio. From fifteen to twenty miles above the mouth of the latter river, then called the Wabash by the French, or within eighty miles or so of their destination, when they were counting the hours to their glad arrival there, they were waylaid by the merciless savages, the mother, son, and two daughters killed, and the father and two servants taken captives. One daughter appears, from other minutes in these records, to have escaped this catastrophe, and she became the wife of the young ensign, Jean B. Girardot, whose signature becomes so familar to us as we turn these ancient pages. There follows another solemn service for Jean B. Robillard, who died and was buried at Point Coupée, upon the Mississippi, the 14th of July of the year 1722, and then the death of Pierre Barel, a married man having wife and children in Canada.

The register is kept entirely by Father Beaubois during these years, except one entry by Boullenger, who states that he made it for Beaubois in his absence, which words are heavily underlined. As he inserts this in the wrong place, by order of dates, and styles it an omission, it is a wonder that Beaubois permitted it to remain. And we can but be thankful that he did not lose his temper on his return, and suppress all that had gone before on this account.

In 1724, the simple relation of what happened in a single day gives us a graphic picture of the sad scenes the infant settlement had sometimes to witness. In that year, "the 12th of April, were slain at break of day by the Fox Indians four men, to-wit: Pierre Du Vaud, a married man about twenty-five years of age, Pierre Bascau dit Beau Soleil, also a married man about 28 or 30 years of age, and two others, of whom one was known by the name of the Bohemian, and the other by the name of L'Etreneusieu, the three last dwelling and employed at Fort de Chartres. Their bodies, having been brought to Cascaskia the same day by the French, were buried at sunset in the cemetery of this parish." From break of day to set of sun! These four, who perhaps had just begun their daily labor in the forest or the fields, were set upon in the early morning by the wily savages, who had come from the far away Fox villages in quest of scalps, and made good their retreat with their trophies, before the sad news was known at the stronghold where the victims dwelt, or at the little village which gave them sepulchre before the evening shades had fallen. It is interesting to notice also that one of these men was called *the Bohemian*, probably the first of that race who came to Illinois, and the earliest use of the name in the annals of the West. September 15, 1725, is mentioned the death of Martha, daughter of M. Girardot, "*officier des troupes*," and of Theresa Nepven, his wife. In 1726, inserted in this burial register are the baptisms of a negress and negro belonging to residents of the village, and in 1727, that of a slave of the Padoucah tribe of Indians. These, with others following, seem to refer to baptisms performed during fatal illness, and hence included in the list of deaths. The attention is attracted by the larger handwriting, and the crosses and heavy lines in the margin of the last entry in this burial register, which reads: "On the 18th of December, 1727, died Zebedeé Le Jeune Donné, of the Reverend Jesuit Fathers, having received the sacraments, and was buried in the parish church, under the second bench from the middle.   The same day were transferred from the old chapel to the said church the bodies of the Reverend Fathers Gabriel Marest and Jean Mermet, religious priests of the Company of Jesus, Missionaries to the Illinois, who died at the said mission." Thus we learn that Marest, one of the founders of Kaśkaskia, and Mermet, who likewise was most intimately associated with the early history of the place, both labored there until the end, and found there a grave.   The good shepherds, who had followed their wandering flock from the banks of the Illinois to a home by the Mississippi, and had seen the roving mission change to a permanent settlement, where they had toiled long and zealously, were buried first in the mission chapel.   But when this structure had fallen into decay, and a new edifice had taken its place, loving hands reverently brought thither the precious dust, that the faithful pastors might still sleep in the midst of their own people.

The record of the deaths occurring in the parish, between the termination of this register in 1727 and the commencement of the burial register opened in 1764, has disappeared.   After the first burial register, and in the same book, is a portion of the first marriage register of the parish, which begins abruptly in 1724, with the nuptials of Antoine and Marie, slaves of the Reverend Fathers the Jesuits.   Among the witnesses who sign, are Girardot, who seems as ready to officiate at a wedding as at a christening, Zebedée Le Jeune, the priest whose death in 1727 is noted in the burial register, and one Francoisé, the last name not given, who makes a mark we think we recognize, and who does not seem to be at all deterred from offering her services as a witness by her inability to write her name.   The same year was the marriage of the widow of a sergeant of the king's miners, which Girardot witnesses, and that of a Frenchman, a widower, to an Indian woman, the widow of Charles Danis.   This seems to have been a notable wedding, and D'Artaguiette and Legardeur de L'Isle sign among the witnesses, and the inevitable Francoise le Brise makes her mark.   Then follows the marriage of a native of Brittany with Anne, a female savage of the Nachitoches tribe, which both Girardot and Francoise le Brise grace with their presence; and the next year, that of a Frenchman with a German woman, which seems to have attracted the attention of the Aborigines, as two chiefs, one the head of the Tamaroa tribe, make their marks as witnesses.   In 1726, Jacques Hyacinthe, of the Pawnee nation, was married to Therese, a freed savage woman of the Padoucah tribe, and the whole party signed with their marks.

Turn we now to another entry of which the handwriting, clear as copper-plate, and the ink almost as dark as if used but yesterday, make it well-nigh impossible to realize that more than one hundred and fifty years have passed since the characters were formed, and the event described took place. It tells us that in the year 1727, the twentieth day of the month of October, the nuptial benediction was pronounced over two inhabitants of the parish, Joseph Lorrin and Marie Philippe, and shows that this was a great social event in the early day. Chassin of the Royal India Company, Girardot, Pierre de Franchomme, and others of the gentry of Kaskaskia sign the register as witnesses, and then appear two signatures, distinct and bold as though freshly written, which we have not met with hitherto. These are the names of Vinsenne and St. Ange fils; the Chevalier Vinsenne, commandant of the post by the Wabash, on the site of which the city of Vincennes, in Indiana, bearing a name derived from his, has grown up, and the young St. Ange, one of his officers, a relative doubtless of the sterling soldier, who was to be the last French Commandant of the Illinois. They had come from their distant station, the nearest neighbor of Kaskaskia, a hundred leagues, in bark canoes, or had traversed the prairie and threaded the forest for days together, to greet old friends and new, and to dance gaily at the wedding, all unmindful of the sad fate to which they were doomed; for, ere ten years passed by, these two, with the knightly D'Artaguiette and the heroic Jesuit Senat, were to perish at the stake among the savage Chickasaws, who wondered to see the white men die so bravely.

The last entry in this marriage record is under date of June 7th, 1729, and for a space of nearly twelve years, or until January 3d, 1741, there is no register of marriages in this parish extant, and the book containing the intervening entries has probably been destroyed. On the day last mentioned it begins again, with R. Tartarin as Curé, and from that time on it is kept in a folio volume of 220 pages, apparently containing a complete record of the marriages at Kaskaskia, from 1741 to 1835. In November, 1741, is noted the marriage of the widow of Pierre Groson de Ste. Ange, lieutenant of a company detached from the marine, perhaps the young officer who died with D'Artaguiette five years before. September 19th, 1746, Father P. J. Watrin becomes Curé, and about this period the names of natives of Quebec and of Detroit, residing at Kaskaskia, frequently occur in the register. Brother Charles Magendie, of the Company of Jesus, acts as assistant to Father Watrin, and we hear also of Monseigneur Mercier, Vicaire General, who occasionally exercises his authority. Slaves, red and black, and freed men and freed women of both colors, give light and shade to the good father's pages, and are dismissed with brief mention. But when, on Jan.

7th, 1748, the wedding of Monsieur Joseph Buchet, exercising the functions of Principal Secretary of the Marine, Sub-delegate of Monsieur the Commissary Ordonnateur and Judge at the Illinois, once a widower, and Marie Louise Michel, twice a widow, is celebrated, and the Reverend Father Guyenne, Superior of the Missions of the Company of Jesus in Illinois, performs the ceremony, assisted, as we should say, by the priest of the parish, the entry is thrice as long as usual. And the Chevalier de Bertel, Major commanding for the King at Fort Chartres, and Benoist de St. Clair, Captain commanding at Kaskaskia, sign the record, and others of the first circles of Kaskaskia, and all are able to write their names. Then follows the wedding of the daughter of Sieur Leonard Billeront, Royal Notary at the Illinois, with the son of Charles Vallée, another name known long and well at Kaskaskia.

In this year, Father S. L. Meurin, who describes himself as a missionary priest of the Company of Jesus, exercising the functions of Curé, signs one marriage entry; and the next year Father M. T. Fourré officiates at the wedding of two slaves of Mr. de Montchevaux, Captain commanding at the Cascaskias. And January 13th, 1750, Father Watrin performed the ceremony at the union of Jean Baptiste Benoist de St. Claire, Captain of infantry, who had now become commandant at the Illinois, and Marie Bienvenue, daughter of Antoine Bienvenue, Major of militia, who had not long before removed from New Orleans to Kaskaskia, where his decendants still reside. And the same year De Giradot signs once more as a witness. In 1751, there appears the name of St. Gemme, which later was prominent in the history of the place. When the property of the Jesuits in Kaskaskia was sold by the French commandant for the crown, under the royal decree for the suppression of the order, St. Gemme was the purchaser, and he became the richest subject in the village, furnishing to the King's magazines as much as 86,000 weight of flour in a single season, which was only part of one year's harvest. The family came from Beauvais, in France, and its members were often called by the name of that town, but the true patronymic was St. Gemme, which some descendants of that stock to-day write St. James. In 1755, De Girardot's signature greets us again, and for the last time in these records. Aubert, Jesuit, relieves Watrin in 1759, and the succeeding year joins in wedlock Dussault de la Croix, *officier des troupes du Roy*, son of Messire Dessault de la Croix, Chevalier of the military order of St. Louis, and the widow of Antoine de Gruye, Lieutenant of the troops, written permission having been given by Monsieur de Macarty, Major Commandant at the Illinois. One of the witnesses is Neyon de Villier, a bold officer in the old French war, who did much damage on the frontiers of the colonies. He was one of the seven brothers, who all held commissions under King Louis, and was Macarty's successor as Commandant of the Illinois country. April 11th, 1763, the bans of marriage were published for the third time between Messire Philippe Francois de Rastel, "*Chevalier de Rocheblave, officier des troupes de cette colonie, natif de Savournon Diocese de Gap en Dauphiné, fils de Messire Jean Joseph de Rastel, Chevalier Marquis de Rocheblave, Seigneur de Savournon le Bersac place du bourg et de vallée de vitrolles,*" and Michel Marie Dufresne, daughter of Jacques Michel Dufresne, officer of militia of this parish; written permission having been given by Monsieur De Neyon de Villiers, Major Commandant at the country of the Illinois, who signs the register. This Rocheblave, at the transfer of the country by the French to the English, took service under the banner of St. George, and was the last British Commandant of the Illinois, being captured at Fort Gage, on the bluff above Kaskaskia, July 4th, 1778, by the able leader, George Rogers Clark. In 1764, Father Meurin seems to take charge of the parish, which he describes as that of the Immaculate Conception of the holy virgin, Village of Kaskaskias, Country of the Illinois, Province of Louisiana, Diocese of Quebec; and associated with him at times was Brother Luc Collet, Missionary Priest at the Illinois. The sturdy priest, Pierre Gibault, assumes the functions of Curé des Kaskaskias et Vicaire General des Illinois et Tamarois, in 1768, and his bold signature, with its unique flourish, greets us through these records for fifteen years or more. We should know that the man with such a chirography would have been just the one to render the efficient assistance given to George Rogers Clark, and must have belonged to the church militant. He was very slow to recognize the change in the civil government of the country, when it was ceded by France to England, which was quite distasteful to him, and hardly notices it in these records. But in 1776, when the Vicar-General of the Illinois country, the former curé, S. L. Meurin, officiated, we find this transfer indicated in the mention of Mr. Hugh Lord, Captain commanding for his Britannic Majesty, and his signature and those of some of his officers are subscribed to one entry. In May, 1778, Father Gibault condescends to speak of Mr. De Rocheblave as Commandant-in-Chief in the country of the Illinois, but does not say under which king; and before he made the next entry, 4th August of same year, the hapless Rocheblave, to Gibault's great satisfaction, was on his way to Virginia, a prisoner of war, and Clark and his "Long Knives," as his men were called, held the fort.

2

Reluctantly we see the last of the handwriting of this friend of the new republic, which is followed in 1785, by that of De Saint Pierre as Curé, and De la Valinière as Vicar-General; and in their time, from 1792 onward, English names begin to appear, such as Archibald McNabb, of Aberdeen, and William St. Clair, son of James St. Clair, captain in the Irish Brigade in the service of France, and John Edgar, once an English officer, and afterward a prominent citizen of Kaskaskia and of Illinois, and Rachel Edgar, his American wife, who persuaded him to forswear the King of Great Britain and all his works; and William Morrison, who emigrated from Philadelphia, in 1790, to establish a mercantile business in the old French town. And with these are the new French names, representing the arrivals from Canada during that period, and noticeable among them that of Pierre Menard, afterwards the first Lieutenant-Governor of Illinois, the son of a liberty-loving Canadian, who fought by the side of Montgomery, at Quebec. In 1793, Gabriel Richard takes up the record as parish priest. Later he was stationed at Detroit, and took a leading part in the early history of Michigan, representing that Territory in Congress, and was the only Catholic priest who was ever a member of that body.

The register runs on without a break well into the present century, and we note as we pass the marriage on May 22d, 1806, of Pierre Menard, widower, and Angelique Saucier, granddaughter of Jean B. Saucier, once a French officer at Fort Chartres, who resigned and settled in the Illinois country. Donatien Ollivier was the officiating priest. In 1817, at the wedding of a daughter of William Morrison, Ninian Edwards, then Governor of the Territory of Illinois, afterward third Governor of the State, and Shadrach Bond, first Governor of the State, sign as witnesses. July 11, 1819, at the marriage of a son of Pierre Chouteau to a daughter of Pierre Menard, it is recited that the husband was born at St. Louis in the Missouri Territory, and the wife at Kaskaskia in the State of Illinois, which is the first mention of the State of Illinois in these records. Many members of these two families, both prominent in the early history of the Illinois country, witness this entry. In April, 1820, William Morrison, Eliza, his wife, Governor Shadrach Bond, and William H. Brown, in after years a leading citizen of Chicago, appear as witnesses, and the last entry in this book, commenced in 1741, is made in 1820. A smaller volume in the same cover continues the list of marriages to 1835, and in a clerkly hand, Sidney Breese, late Chief-Justice of the Supreme Court of Illinois, affixes his signature to an entry made February 11th, 1822. John Reynolds, afterwards Governor of Illinois, is a witness in 1824, and two years later, Felix St. Vrain, the Indian agent, murdered by the savages at the outbreak of the Black-Hawk war, signs the record, and with him Nathaniel Pope, delegate to Congress from the Territory of Illinois, and first United States Judge for the District of Illinois—all in the time of Francois Xavier Dahmen, priest of the Congregation.

In a folio volume, imported, as it would appear, from Bordeaux, the Register of Baptisms is resumed in 1759, and continued to 1801, and is carried on in a smaller volume to 1815. One of its many curious entries is of the baptism of "the son of an infidel savage woman of the Choctaw tribe, and a savage man of the Peorias;" and numerous baptisms among negro slaves take place.

In a smaller book, the Burial Register begins again with this statement, "The old register of persons deceased in the Parish of the Immaculate Conception of the Kaskaskias having been filled, I have continued to register in the old book of accounts, of which a large part was blank. The Register of Deaths commencing only at this leaf, the 8th day of September, 1764." Of the old register, thus referred to, which probably filled the gap from Dec. 18th, 1727, to September 8th, 1764, no trace can be discovered, and it is probably destroyed. One of the first entries in 1764, by Father Meurin, is of the death and burial of a poor voyageur, of whom he says: "I know neither the family, nor the parish, nor where or when he was born." Some years later, Father G.'s vault buries a little Illinois savage eight hours after baptism; and in 1779, a negro slave belonging to "Mr. Le Colonel Klark." And the same year, he performs the funeral service over Joseph Brayeau, aged seventy-eight years, slain the night before, by the savages on the Kaskaskia River. He also buries two little Illinois savages, one named Francois and the other Michael, and, shortly after, holds a solemn service for Charles Robbin, native of Canada, aged about thirty-eight years, killed by the savages, at the point of the River of the Kaskaskias; "his body was found and buried on an island of the Mississippi." He next chants a solemn service in memory of Joseph Bineau, a young man from Detroit, slain on the banks of the Beautiful River by the savages with four other Frenchmen in the same canoe. And the following year, one is sung for the repose of the soul of Jean De Noyon, slain by the savages on the Beautiful River, and buried on L'Isle aux Boeufs "by all those who belonged to the barge who have certified that they were present at his death, and at that of Joseph la Fleur, killed and buried with him." It appears that the Indians did not always confine themselves to white victims, for he records the death of one named Pierre, an Illinois indian, killed by his enemies along the River of the Kaskaskias. In 1792, died Archibald McNabb, native of the Shire of Perth, in Scotland, and next is mentioned the killing of two men, from the village of Kaskaskia, who fell by the hand of the savages upon the River Cumberland or Shawanon. In 1827, the death of a slave of Mr. Cain is noted. Probably Elias K. Kane is referred to, one of the first senators from Illinois. And we learn, at this last date, that Kaskaskia has ceased to be a part of the diocese of Quebec, and now belongs to that of Baltimore.

We might continue thus to cull from these old records things grave and gay, quaint and interesting, but the limits of this paper compel us to forbear, and we must leave the greater part of them untouched. It is pleasant to pour over the brown pages, to decipher the cramped handwriting, and to imagine the long succession of worthy priests making their careful entries, little thinking that they would ever be read beyond the bounds of their own parish, or be of value to any but the dwellers therein, but they made them none the less faithfully. And so these parish records, intended simply to show the births, marriages, and deaths among the people of one little village, for the greater part of its existence an outpost of civilization in the heart of the western wilderness, unconsciously and so most accurately reveal much of the early history of the region which is now a great State.

They tell us of the black-robed missionaries, who made those long and weary journeys to plant the cross among the savages, and toiled to spread their faith with a zeal and devotion unsurpassed; of the bold pioneers, who, for the sake of gain and adventure, traversed the wilds with their lives in their hands and of their merciless foes; of the days of wild speculation, when the streets of Paris were full of eager purchasers of shares in the wonder-working company which was to found an empire on the banks of the Mississippi, and draw endless riches from the mines to be opened there; of the high-born officers, who sought distinction or promotion by service in this far-away colony, and of their soldiers, trained to war across the sea; and, as we read, plumes and banners wave, and sabres clank, and the red men look curiously at the musketeers, and those whose names are written in the pages of these time-worn books pass before us, and the old scenes come back again. They give us glimpses too of the struggle between two mighty nations for the valley of the Beautiful River, and for dominion in the New World, the prelude to the mightier struggle in which the victor in the earlier strife lost its conquests and its ancient possessions as well; and of the part which this early settlement played in those contests. We see the sceptre pass from one nation to another, and when the sound of war is hushed we note the coming of peace, with commerce and agriculture in its train. And, as the tide of enterprise reaches the old French village, we see its temporary transformation into an American town, and can realize its astonishment at finding its limits extending, its population doubling, its streets thronged, and itself the seat of government of a vast territory and the first capital of a State. And we can appreciate its relief when the wave recedes and the new names disappear, and rejoice with it that this episode is over, and it is left to its ancient ways and its own familiar people, and to a rest which has since been almost undisturbed.

And hence, for one who approaches it to-day, there is little to disturb the impression that it is really the Kaskaskia of the olden time to which he draws near. The way still lies, as of yore, through a forest, in which stands the old residence of Pierre Menard, vacant, and fast going to decay, but with its furniture and books still in place, as if its occupants of long ago had left but yesterday. It is a type of the village itself, once astir with life, now full of stillness. As you cross the Kaskaskia River by the old-fashioned ferry, and are greeted by the ancient ferryman, the illusion is not dispelled. And the wide streets, unmarked by wheel-tracks; the antique French houses, with their high dormer-windows; the old brick buildings, the first erected of that material in Illinois, each with a history—this one the earliest court-house in the State, and that one the old United States land-office —built of three-inch bricks, brought from Pittsburg in flatboats, in 1792; the priest's house, constructed of materials from the ruins of the nunnery once located there; and the parish church, containing the bell cast at Rochelle, in France, in 1741, for this parish, the first that rang between the Alleghanies and the Mississippi—all give one a mingled impression of antiquity and departed greatness.

You may dine at the village tavern, in the same great room, fully thirty feet square, in which dinner was served to the Marquis de Lafayette, in 1825, when he tarried here on his way down the Mississippi, and note the quaint wood-carving of the high mantlepiece, and of the mouldings of the doors and windows, and see beneath the porch the heavy hewn timbers of which the house is built, justifying the tradition that it is a century and a-quarter old, and was already venerable when Edward Coles, the second Governor of Illinois, made it his residence. You may see part of the foundation of the William Morrison house, at which a reception was given to Lafayette, and the dilapidated framework of the Edgar mansion, where he was a guest. The site of the house of the French commandant, which was afterwards the first

State House of Illinois, will be pointed out to you, and the place where stood the nunnery, and such landmarks as the corner-stone of the property of the Jesuits confiscated by the French Crown, and the post of Cahokia Gate, once giving passage through the fence that bounded the Common Fields, which are still divided and held by the old French measurement and title. And you will learn that the little village, now containing less than three hundred souls, is the owner of some eleven thousand acres of the most fertile land in the Valley of the Mississippi, under the grant to it of Kaskaskia Commons, by his Most Christian Majesty Louis the XV., in 1725, and derives therefrom abundant revenue. The older residents will talk to you of the flood of 1784, of which they have heard their fathers tell; and of Lafayette's visit, which they remember as boys, when, perched on the fence, they saw the stately form, in foreign garb, pass into the Edgar mansion, or peered at him through the windows as he sat at dinner in the large room of the tavern; and of the great flood of 1844, when the water was five feet deep above the floors of their houses, and large steamboats came up the Kaskaskia River and through the streets of the village, and, gathering the terror-stricken inhabitants from trees and roofs, went straight away across the Common Fields to the Mississippi. Of more modern events they have little to say, nor do the later years furnish them topics to take the place of these.

The little community, content to believe itself the first permanent European settlement in the Valley of the Mississippi, sleeps on, dreaming of its early days and of its former importance. It pays little heed to the warnings which the mighty river has already given it, and is seemingly unmindful that the third and last is at hand. The distance from the village centre to the the river bank, once three miles, has been reduced one-half, and the rich farm lands, which once bordered the stream, have gone in its current to the Gulf of Mexico. And now the Mississippi, unsatisfied even with this rapid destruction, in the very wantonness of its strength has cut its way above the town towards the Kaskaskia River, despite the efforts of the Government engineers to check it, until but a space of three hundred yards separates the two. The grave of Illinois' first Governor has been disturbed, and but recently his remains were removed to a safer resting-place. And when the junction is made, the united rivers at the next flood-time will spare nothing of the ancient village, which meanwhile listens idly to the murmur of the approaching waters, and smiles in the shadow of its impending doom, which, before another spring has passed, may be so complete that there will remain no memento of Kaskaskia save its old Parish Records.

OLD FORT CHARTRES.

A Paper read before the Chicago Historical Society, June 16, 1880.

THE marvellous growth of the Great West obscures all relating to it, save what is of recent date. It has a past and a history, but these are hidden by the throng of modern events. Few realize that the territory of Illinois, which seems but yesterday to have passed from the control of the red man to that of our Republic, was once claimed by Spain, occupied by France, and conquered by England. And fewer still, may know that within its boundaries yet remain the ruins of a fortress, in its time the most formidable in America, which filled a large place in the operations of these great powers in the valley of the Mississippi. Above the walls of old Fort Chartres, desolate now, and almost forgotten, have floated, in turn, the flags of two mighty nations, and its story is an epitome of their strife for sovereignty over the New World.

The union of Canada, by a line of forts, with the region of the West and South, was a favorite scheme of the French crown at an early day. It originated in the active brain of the great explorer, LaSalle, whose communications to the ministers of Louis XIV. contain the first suggestions of such a policy. These military stations were intended to be centres of colonization for the vast inland territory, and its protection against rival nations. Spain laid claim to nearly the whole of North America, under the name of Florida, by the right of first discovery, and by virtue of a grant from the Pope, who disposed of a continent—which he did not own—with reckless liberality. France relied on the possession taken by LaSalle for her title to the Mississippi Valley; and a long altercation ensued. The ordinary state of feeling between their officers may be inferred from a correspondence which has come down to us from the early part of the eighteenth century. Bernard de la Harpe established a French post on the Red River, and this aroused the ire of Don Martin de la Come, the nearest Spanish commandant. Writes the Spaniard: "I am compelled to say that your arrival surprises me very much.

Your governor could not be ignorant that the post you occupy belongs to my government. I counsel you to give advice of this to him, or you will force me to oblige you to abandon lands that the French have no right to occupy. I have the honor to be, Sir, &c., De la Come." To him replies the courteous Frenchman: "Permit me to inform you that M. de Bienville is perfectly informed of the limits of his government, and is very certain that this post depends not upon the dominions of his catholic majesty. If you will do me the favor to come into this quarter, I will convince you I hold a post I know how to defend. I have the honor to be, Sir, &c., De la Harpe."

Here and elsewhere, the French held their own, and continued to occupy the disputed territory. In the Illinois country, the mission villages of Cahokia and Kaskaskia sprang up and throve apace. From the latter place, as early as 1715, the good father Mermet reported to the Governor of Canada that the encroaching English were building forts near the Ohio and the Mississippi. So the shadow of the coming power of her old enemy was cast athwart the path of France in the Western wilderness, while Spain watched her progress there with a jealous eye. And the need of guarding the Illinois settlements became more manifest when the discovery of valuable mines in that locality was announced. Such rumors often repeated, and the actual smelting of lead on the west bank of the Mississippi, had their effect in the Mother Country. And when the grant of the province of Louisiana to the merchant Crozat, was surrendered, in 1717, John Law's famous Company of the West, afterward absorbed in that of the Indies, was ready to become his successor, and to dazzle the multitude with the glittering lure of the gold and silver of Illinois. The representatives of this great corporation, in unison with those of the French crown, recognizing the many reasons for a military post in that far-away region, made haste to found it; and thus Fort Chartres arose. It was established as a link in the great chain of strongholds, which was to stretch from the St. Lawrence to the Gulf, realizing the dream of LaSalle; a bulwark against Spain and a barrier to England; a protector of the infant colony, and of the church which planted it; a centre for trade, and for the operation of the far-famed mines; and as the chief seat in the New World of the Royal Company of the Indies, which wove a spell so potent that its victims saw, in the near future, crowded cities all along the course of the Mississippi, and stately argosies afloat upon its waters, one hundred and fifty years ago.

On the 9th of February, 1718, there arrived at Mobile, by

ship, from France, Pierre Duqué Boisbriant, a Canadian gentleman, with the commission of Commandant at the Illinois. He
was a cousin of Bienville, then Governor of Louisiana, and had
already served under him in that province. In October, of the
same year, accompanied by several officers and a detachment of
troops, he departed for the Illinois country, where he was ordered
to construct a fort. The little flotilla, stemming the swift current
of the Mississippi, moved slowly on its way, encountering no
enemies more troublesome than "the mosquitoes, which," says
the worthy priest Poisson, who took the same journey shortly
after, "have caused more swearing since the French have been
here, than had previously taken place in all the rest of the
world." Late in the year, Boisbriant reached Kaskaskia, and
selected a site for his post sixteen miles above that village, on the
left bank of the Mississippi. Merrily rang the axes of the
soldiers in the forest by the mighty river, as they hewed out the
ponderous timbers for palisade and bastion. And by degrees
the walls arose, and the barracks and commandant's house, and
the store-house and great hall of the India Company were built,
and the cannon, bearing the insignia of Louis XIV., were placed
in position. In the spring of 1720, all was finished, the banner
of France was given to the breeze, and the work was named
Fort Chartres. An early governor of the State of Illinois, who
wrote its pioneer history, has gravely stated that this Fort was
so called, because it had a charter from the crown of France for
its erection. But it is feared that the same wag who persuaded
an Illinois legislature to name the second capital of the State,
Vandalia, by reason of the alleged traces of a tribe of Indians
named the Vandals in the neighborhood of the site, also victim-
ized a governor. We can hardly accept his derivation, when it
seems so much more probable that the name was taken, by way
of compliment to the then Regent, from the title of his son, the
Duc de Chartres, for whom, about this time, streets were named
in New Orleans and Kaskaskia, which are still thus designated.

The first important arrival at the new post was that of Philip
Francis Renault, formerly a banker in Paris, the director-general
of the mines of the India Company, who reached Fort Chartres
before its completion, and made his headquarters there. He
brought with him 250 miners and soldiers, and also a large
number of slaves from St. Domingo. This was the beginning of
negro slavery in Illinois. The practice of enslaving Indian
captives was already in vogue, but from this time on, the records
of the French settlements there, speak of both black slaves, and
red slaves. The Fort was finished not at all too soon. The

tardy Spaniards had at last decided to strike a blow at their neighbor on the Mississippi, and Boisbriant hardly had everything in readiness, when news reached him of the march of a force from Mexico against his stronghold.   But this invasion was repelled by the natives on the route, and all concerned in it slain, except the chaplain of the expedition, who was taken prisoner by the Pawnees.   He finally escaped in a dexterous manner.   While delighting the Indians with feats of horseman· ship, he gradually withdrew to a distance, and described a final elaborate figure which had no return curve.   Two Indian chiefs, who displayed, as trophies, a Catalonian pistol and a pair of Spanish shoes, gave this account to Father Charlevoix, at Green Bay.

This pleasant old traveler was then making the journey through North America, of which he has left such a charming account. On the 9th of October, 1721, he passed Fort Chartres, which stood a musket-shot from the river, as he tells us, and he further says, "M. Duqué de Boisbriant commands here for the Company to whom the place belongs.   The French are now beginning to settle the country between this Fort and Kaskaskia."   The leader of Charlevoix' escort was a young Canadian officer, Jean St. Ange de Belle Rive, destined in later years to have a closer acquaintance with Fort Chartres than this passing glimpse of its newly-built walls and structures afforded him.   He hardly anticipated then that to him would come the honor of commanding it, and that on him, almost half a century later, would fall the sad duty of finally lowering there his country's flag, which waved so proudly above it on that autumn morning.

No sooner was the Fort erected, than a village began to grow up at its gates, in which the watchful Jesuits forthwith established the parish of Sainte Anne de Fort Chartres.   All that remains of the records of this parish, is in the writer's possession.   They begin with an ancient document, tattered and worn, written in Quebec, in the year 1716.   It is a copy of a curious decree of Louis XV., promulgated in the same year, which seems to be something in the nature of a manual of church etiquette.   Reciting that his majesty has considered all the ordinances on the subject of honors in the churches of New France, and wishes to put an end to all the contests on the subject, it proceeds to regulate the whole matter.   Twelve articles provide that the governor-general and the intendant shall each have a prie Dieu in the cathedrals of Quebec and Montreal, the governor-general on the right, the intendant on the left; the commander of the troops shall have a seat behind the governor-general; in church-processions, the governor-general shall march at the head of the council, his guards in front, the intendant to the left and behind the council, and the chief notary, first usher, and captain of the guard, with the governor-general, yet behind him, but not on the same line with the council; and similar minute directions cover all contingencies. In all other churches of New France, the same rules of precedence are to be observed according to the rank of those in attendance. Doubtless, copies of this important decree were kept in readiness, that one might be furnished to each new church at its establishment. And probably the one from which we quote was sent from Quebec to Ste. Anne of Fort Chartres some time in 1721, the year in which the first entries seem to have been made in the parish registers. We may presume that Boisbriant followed its instructions strictly, and took care to be on the right hand in the church, and also that the intendant or civil officer should be on the left. That position was filled by Marc Antoine de la Loire. des Ursins, principal director for the Company of the Indies. These two, together with Michel Chassin, commissary for the Company, formed the Provincial Council of the Illinois, and speedily made Fort Chartres the centre of the civil government of the colony. To this council applications for land were made, and its members executed the grants upon which many titles rest to this day. Boisbriant, doubtless believing that he that provideth not for his own household is worse than an infidel, had a large tract conveyed to himself, beginning at the little hill behind the Fort. He and his associates dispensed justice, regulated titles, and administered estates, and, in fact, established the court, which, for more than forty years, decided the causes which arose in the Illinois country, according to the civil law. Their largest land grant was made in 1723, to M. Renault, and comprised a tract west of the Mississippi, another, fifteen leagues square, near the site of Peoria, and another above Fort Chartres, one league along the river and two leagues deep, the latter to raise provisions for his settlements among the mines. Of this last tract, a large part was never sold by Renault, and to this day the unconveyed portion is marked upon the maps of Monroe County, Ill., as the property of the Philip Renault heirs.

About this time word came to the Fort that the faithful allies of the French, the Illinois Indians, who dwelt about Peoria Lake, and the Rock of St. Louis, now called Starved Rock, were hard pressed by their ancient enemies, the Foxes. Boisbriant sent a force to their relief which arrived at the close of a contest, in which the Foxes were defeated, but so greatly had the Illinois.

suffered that they returned with the French to the shelter of the Fort, leaving the route to the settlements from the north unprotected. In the year 1725, Bienville, the Governor of Louisiana, was summoned to France, and Commandant Boisbriant became acting Governor in his stead, with headquarters at New Orleans. His old position was filled by M. De Siette, a captain in the royal army. In the parish register in his administration, appears the baptism of a female savage of the Padoucah nation, by the chaplain at the Fort, who records with great satisfaction that he performed the ceremony, and gave her the name of Therese, but does not say whether she consented, or what she thought about it. She apparently paid a casual visit to the Fort, and he baptized her at a venture, and made haste to write down another convert. The Fox Indians were a thorn in the side of De Siette. The way by the Illinois River was now open to them, and their war parties swooped upon the settlers, murdering them in their fields, even within a few miles of the Fort. In great wrath, De Siette opened a correspondence on the subject with De Lignerie, the French commandant at Green Bay, and proposed that the Fox tribe should be exterminated at once. The calmer De Lignerie, replies in substance that this would be the best possible expedient, provided the Foxes do not exterminate them in the attempt. And he suggests a postponement of hostilities until De Siette and himself could meet "*at Chickagau or the Rock,*" and better concert their plans. But soon the French authorities adoped the views of the commandant at the Illinois, and the Marquis de Beauharnois, grandfather of the first husband of the Empress Josephine, then commanding in Canada, notified him to join the Canadian forces at Green Bay, in 1728, to make war upon the Foxes. A battle ensued, in which the Illinois Indians, headed by the French, were victorious. But hostilities continued until De Siette's successor, by a masterly piece of strategy, waylaid and destroyed so many of the persistent foemen, that peace reigned for a time.

This officer, M. de St. Ange de Belle Rive, who, as we have seen, first visited the Illinois country with Father Charlevoix, had since been stationed there, and made it his home, for the ancient title records of this region show that in 1729 he purchased a house in the prairie bounding on one side the road leading to Fort Chartres. And in an old package of stained and mouldering papers, but lately disinterred from the dust of at least one century, is the original petition addressed by St. Ange to the proper authorities for the confirmation of his title to certain land, not far from the Fort, acquired "from *a savage named Chicago,*

who is contented and satisfied with the payment made to him."
During his term of office, in 1732, the Royal India Company
surrendered its charter to the crown, which thenceforward had the
exclusive government of the country. A few years before, the
French warfare with the Natchez Indians, that strange tribe of
sun-worshippers, probably of the Aztec race, had resulted in the
dispersion of the natives, some of whom joined the Chickasaws,
who, under English influence, kept up the strife. A young
officer, Pierre D'Artaguiette, distinguished himself so greatly in
the Natchez war, that he was appointed to the Illinois district,
in 1734, taking the place of St. Ange, who was transferred to
another post. The new commander was a younger brother of
Diron D'Artaguiette, a man very prominent in the early history of
Louisiana, and his family connections, his services and virtues,
his brilliant career and untimely death, have surrounded his
name with a halo of romance. With pride and pleasure, he
received his promotion to the rank of major, and his orders
to take command at Fort Chartres. For two years he ruled
his province well, and then the summons to the field came
to him again. Bienville had resumed the Governorship and
resolved to crush the Chickasaws. In preparation for the
campaign he strengthened all the posts, that they might better
spare a part of their garrisons for active work. De Coulanges,
.an officer sent to Fort Chartres with a supply of ammunition,
disobeyed orders, transporting merchandise instead, leaving the
powder at the Arkansas. A party of D'Artaguiette's men going
after it, was routed by the Chickasaws. "For this," Bienville
says, "I have ordered D'Artaguiette to imprison De Coulanges
for six months in Fort Chartres. I hope this example will
moderate the avidity for gain of some of our officers." When
everything was in readiness, D'Artaguiette set forth from Fort
Chartres with all his force, on a morning in February, making a
brave show as the fleet of bateaux and canoes floated down the
Mississippi. This first invasion of Southern soil by soldiers from
Illinois, comprised nearly all of the garrison of the Fort, a company of volunteers from the French villages, almost the whole of
the Kaskaskia tribe, and a throng of Indian warriors who had
flocked to the standard even from the far away Detroit. Chicago
led the Illinois and the Miamis, and at the mouth of the Ohio,
the Chevalier Vinsenne joined the expedition, with the garrison
from the post on the Wabash, and a number of Indians, including
a party of Iroquois braves. Landing, and marching inland, they
reached the Chickasaw villages at the appointed time, but the
troops from New Orleans, who were to meet them there, failed to

appear.   Compelled to fight or retreat, D'Artaguiette chose the former, and was at first successful, but the tide turned, when he fell, covered with wounds.   De Coulanges, released from durance that he might redeem his fame, and many other officers, were slain, most of the Indians fled, and D'Artaguiette, Vinsenne, the Jesuit Senat, and young St. Ange, son of the Illinois command-ant, were taken prisoners by the unconquered Chickasaws, who burned them at the stake, and triumphantly marched to the Georgia coast to tell their English allies there of the French defeat.   The broken remnants of the little army, under the leadership of a boy of sixteen, pursued by the savages for five and twenty leagues, regained the river, and slowly and sadly returned to the Fort.   On the sorrow caused there by the mournful news, the masses that were said in the little church for the repose of the souls of the slain, and the deep grief felt throughout the country of the Illinois, in cabin and wigwam alike, we will not dwell.   The impression made by the life and death of D'Artaguiette was so abiding, that his name remained a household word among the French for years; and well into the present century, the favorite song among the negroes along the Mississippi was one, of which the oft-repeated chorus ran,

> "In the days of D'Artaguiette, Ho! Ho!
> In the days of D'Artaguiette, O ho!"

Three years later, La Buissoniére, who succeeded him, led an expedition from Fort Chartres, composed of Frenchmen and natives, to take part in another campaign against the dauntless Chickasaws.   Soldiers from Quebec and Montreal, with recruits from all the tribes along their route, overtook him on the way, and the Northern forces joined the troops under Bienville, newly reinforced from Paris, near the site of the city of Memphis. The dominions of the King of France, in the Old World and the New, were laid under contribution to concentrate this army at the rendezvous, but not a blow was struck.   White and red men lay in camp for months, apparently unwilling to risk an encounter, and at length a dubious peace was arranged, and all marched home again, without loss or glory.   Hardly had the Fort-Chartres detachment returned, when a boat, going from New Orleans to the Illinois, was attacked by the Chickasaws, above the mouth of the Ohio, and all on board were killed, save one young girl.   She had recently arrived from France, and was on her way to join her sister, the wife of an officer at the Fort.   Escaping by a miracle to the shore, she wandered through the woods for days, living on herbs, until sore spent and ready to die, she chanced to reach an elevation from which she caught a glimpse of the flag floating over Fort Chartres, and, with new hope and strength, struggled onward, and came safely to the friends who had mourned for her as dead.

Among the few original documents relating to this period which are still preserved, is a deed executed at Fort Chartres by Alphonse de la Buissoniére, commandant at the Illinois, and Madame Theresa Trudeau, his wife. During his governorship were the halcyon days of the French settlers at the Illinois. The Indians were kept in check, the fertile soil yielded bounteous harvests, two convoys laden with grain and provisions, went each year to New Orleans, and Lower Louisiana became almost entirely dependent upon them for supplies. Other villages had grown up near the Fort. Prairie du Rocher, five miles away, was situated upon a grant made by the India Company to Boisbriant, and by him transferred to his nephew, Langlois, who conveyed it by parcels to the settlers, reserving to himself certain seigneurial rights according to the customs of Paris. And Renault, on a portion of his grant above the Fort, established the village of St. Philip, which became a thriving place. These were laid out after the French manner, with Commons and Common Fields, still marked upon the local maps, and in some cases held and used to this day under the provisions of these early grants. In each of the villages was a chapel, under the jurisdiction of the parent church of Ste. Anne of Fort Chartres. To the colony came scions of noble families of France, seeking fame and adventure in that distant land, and their names and titles appear at length in the old records and parish registers. Among them was Benoist St. Claire, captain of a company detached from the marine service, who followed La Buissoniére in the chief command, and held it for a year or more. He found little to do in those piping times of peace, made an occasional grant of land, and sought other service early in 1742.

The Chevalier de Bertel, who describes himself as Major Commanding for the King, took charge in his stead. The parish register of Ste. Anne, in his time, is extant, and the title-page of the volume, then newly opened, bears the following inscription: "Numbered and initialed by us, Principal Secretary of the Marine and Civil Judge at the Illinois, the present book, containing seventy-four leaves, to serve as a Register of the Parish of St. Anne, of Baptisms, Marriages, and Deaths. Done at Fort Chartres the first of August, 1743.

"CHEVALIER DE BERTEL,   DE LA LOIRE,
          Major Commandant.   FLANCOUR."

The pages which remain, by their careful numbering and joint initials, show how important it was deemed to preserve and identify this register. It was soon to contain the record of the sudden death of Flancour himself, the Civil Judge at the Illinois. One of his last acts was to grant to the village of Prairie du Rocher, a tract of land for Commons, from which it now derives a revenue. And with Bertel he executed a deed to a young man at St. Philip, for the reason that he was the first one born in Illinois to marry and settle himself. And to another, who asked the gift of a farm, because he had seven children, they granted a tract of land for each child. Renault made his last conveyance of a lot at St. Philip by deed, executed in his rooms at Fort Chartres, September 2d, 1740, and, three years later, returned to Paris, after a residence in the Illinois country of nearly a quarter of a century. In the same season, Governor Bienville went to France, finally resigning his trust to the Marquis de Vandreuil. And here a word may be spoken of the first royal governor of the province, of which Illinois was a part, and in whose admin- istration Fort Chartres was constructed. Le Moyne de Bienville, a Canadian born, was one of an illustrious family. His father was killed in battle in the service of his country, seven of his brothers died naval officers, and of the three others, then surviv- ing, one was Governor of Montreal, one captain of a ship of the line, and one a naval ensign. He distinguished himself at the capture of Port Nelson from the English, and in a brilliant naval engagement in Hudson's Bay; was one of the founders of Louisiana; and chose the site of the city of New Orleans. He served as Lieutenant-Governor and Governor of the Province for nearly forty years, and won the reputation of being the bravest and best man in the colony. His portrait, which adorns the mansion, at Longueil, in Canada, of Baron Grant, the repre- sentative of the family, shows a martial figure, and a noble face, in keeping with his record; and his intimate connection with its early history would make it fitting to preserve a copy of this original in the State of Illinois.

The Chevalier de Bertel had a difficult part to play. France and England were at war, because Frederick the Great and Marie Theresa could not agree, and this disturbed the settlements at the Illinois. Some Englishmen, found on the Mississippi, were arrested as spies, and confined in the dungeon as Fort Chartres, and whispers of an English attack were in the air. The Fort was out of repair, and poorly supplied, and a number of its soldiers, tiring of the confinement of the garrison, deserted, to try the free life of the woods and prairies. The old-time Indian allies were won over by the British, and agreed to destroy the French post during the moon of the fall of the leaf, but they were thwarted by the skill and address of De Bertel. Many anxious thoughts he had as he paced the enclosure of Fort Chartres, and many an earnest epistle he addressed to his superior officers, assuring them that it was only by great good fortune that he could hold his post, which must be reënforced and strengthened. The abandonment of the Fort was at one time contemplated. This plan, however, was given up when the Marquis de Galissonière, Gov.-General of Canada, presented a memorial on the subject to the home government. He says, "The little colony of Illinois ought not to be left to perish. The King must sacrifice for its support. The principal advantage of the country is its extreme productiveness, and its connection with Canada and Louisiana must be maintained." The peace of Aix la Chapelle came in time to give both parties a breathing space, in which to prepare for the sterner contest, soon to follow. Chevalier de Bertel, knowing that his wise counsels had borne fruit, transferred the command again to Benoist St. Clair, who signalized his return by wedding the daughter of a citizen of Kaskaskia, in January, 1750. The same year, De Galissonière once more urged upon the King the importance of preserving and strengthening the post at the Illinois, describing the country as open and ready for the plough, and traversed by an innumerable multitude of buffaloes. "And these animals," he says, "are covered with a species of wool, sufficiently fine to be employed in various manufactories!" And he further suggests, and, doubtless, correctly, that "the buffalo, if caught, and attached to the plow, would move it at a speed superior to that of the domestic ox!"

In the succeeding autumn, the Chevalier de Makarty,* a major of engineers, with a few companies of troops, arrived from France, under orders to rebuild the citadel of the Illinois country. Other detachments followed, until nearly a full regiment of French grenadiers answered to the roll-call at Fort Chartres. They toiled busily to transform it from a fortress of wood to one of stone, under the skilful guidance of the trained officer, whose Irish blood, as well as his French commission, made hostile preparations against Britain, a labor of love to him. You may see, to this day, the place in the bluffs to the eastward of the Fort, where they quarried the huge blocks, which they carried in boats

---

* This is the same officer whose name is spelled Macarty in the Parish Records of Kaskaskia. The discovery of the records of the church of St. Anne of Fort Chartres, containing his name, written by himself, shows the proper spelling to be Makarty.

3

across the little lake lying between.   The finer stone, with which
the gateways and buildings were faced, were brought from beyond
the Mississippi.   A million of crowns seemed to the King of
France but a reasonable expense for this work of reconstruction,
which was to secure his empire in the West.   And hardly was it
completed when the contest began, and the garrison of Fort
Chartres had a hand in the opening struggle.   In May, 1754,
the young George Washington, with his Virginia riflemen, surprised the party of Jumonville at the Great Meadows, and slew
the French leader.   His brother, Neyon de Villiers, one of the
captains at Fort Chartres, obtained leave from Makarty to
avenge him, and with his company, went by the Mississippi and
the Ohio, to Fort du Quesne, where he joined the head of the
family, Coulon de Villiers, who was marching on the same errand.
Together, with "a force as numerous," said the Indians, "as the
pigeons in the woods," they brought to bay "Monsieur de Wac-
henston," as the French despatches call him, at Fort Necessity,
which he surrendered on the 4th of July.   The capture of this
place by the French, is one of the causes assigned by George the
Second, for the declaration of hostilities by Britain; and thus
the Old French War began.   The little detachment, with its bold
leader, returned, flushed with victory, to celebrate, at Fort
Chartres, the triumph of Illinois over Virginia.   Soon the
demands upon this post for supplies and men grew constant, and
the veteran Makarty labored steadily to keep pace with them.
The commandant at Fort du Quesne, whose communications
with Canada were interrupted by the British, writes him: "We
are in sad want of provisions.   I send to you for flour and pork."
The Governor-General of Canada, in an epistle to the Minister of
Marine, observes: "I knew the route from the Illinois was as
fine as could be desired.   Chevalier de Villiers, who commands
the escort of provisions from there, came up with a bateaux of
18,000 weight.   This makes known a sure communication with
the Illinois whence I can derive succor in provisions and men."
Nor did our garrison confine itself to commissary work.   The
tireless De Villiers, hardly resting from his escort duty, crossed
the Alleghanies with his men, and captured Fort Granville, on
the Juniata.   The Marquis de Montcalm, writing to the Minister
of War, thus pleasantly alludes to this little attention paid by
Illinois to Pennsylvania: "The news from the Beautiful River is
excellent.   We continue to devastate Pennsylvania.   Chevalier
de Villiers, brother of Jumonville, who was assassinated by the
British, has just burned Fort Granville, sixty miles from Philadelphia."   The next year, Aubry, another of the Fort Chartres

captains, was sent by Makarty, with 400 men, to reënforce Fort du Quesne, then threatened by the British. The morning after his arrival, he sallied out and routed Major Grant and his High-landers, and, a few days later, surprised the British camp forty-five miles away, captured their horses, and brought his party back mounted. Soon, however, the approach of a superior force, with Washington and his riflemen in the van, compelled the abandonment of Fort du Quesne. By the light of its burning stockade, the Illinois troops sailed down the Beautiful River, and sadly returned to their homes.

The British star was now in the ascendant, yet still the French struggled gallantly. Once more the drum beat to-arms on the parade-ground at Fort Chartres, at the command to march to raise the siege of Fort Niagara. All the Illinois villages sent volunteers, and Aubry led the expedition by a devious route, joining the detachments from Detroit and Michi-limackinac, on Lake Erie. As they entered the Niagara River, Indian scouts reported that they were "like a floating island, so black was the stream with their bateaux and canoes." The desperate charge upon the British lines failed, Aubry, covered with wounds, fell into the hands of the enemy, and the bulletin reads, "Of the French from the Illinois, many were killed and many taken prisoner." Despair and gloom settled upon the Fort and its neighborhood, when the sorrowful news came back. Makarty writes to the Governor-General: "The defeat at Niagara has cost me the flower of my men. My garri-son is weaker than ever. The British are building bateaux at Pittsburg. I have made all arrangements, according to my strength, to receive the enemy." And the Governor-General replies, "I strongly recommend you to be on your guard." The surrender, at Montreal, of the Canadas, followed upon the victory on the plains of Abraham, but still the Illinois held out for the King. Neyon de Villiers received his well-earned promotion, and assumed command at Fort Chartres. And the fine old soldier, Makarty, doubtless, regretting that he had not had the opportunity to test the strength of the goodly stone walls he had builded, sheathed his sword, twirled his moustache, made his bow, and departed.

The village at the Fort gate, which, after the rebuilding, was called New Chartres, had become a well-established community. The title records quaintly illustrate its ways of transacting busi-ness, as when, for instance, the royal notary at the Illinois declares that he made a certain public sale in the forenoon of Sunday, after the great parochial mass of St. Anne of New

Chartres, at the main door of the church, offering the property in a high and audible voice, while the people were going out in great numbers from said church. And the parish register, which, briefly and drily, notes the marriages of the common people, spares neither space nor words in the record of the weddings in the families of the officers at the Fort. When Jean la Freilé de Vidrinne, officer of a company, is married to Elizabeth de Moncharveaux, daughter of Jean Francois Liveron de Moncharveaux, captain of a company, and when the Monsieur André Chevalier, royal solicitor and treasurer for the King at the country of the Illinois, weds Madeleine Loisel, names, and titles, and ancestry, are set forth at length, and Makarty, the commandant, Buchet, the principal writer, Du Barry, a lieutenant, all the dignitaries of fort and village, and all the relatives, subscribe the register as witnesses. The ladies sign with a careful deliberation, indicating that penmanship was not one of their recreations; the gentlemen with flourishes so elaborate, that they seem to have been hardly able to bring them to a close. These entries appear in a separate volume, the last in date of the parish books, entitled "Register of the Marriages made in the Parish of St. Anne, containing seventeen sheets, or sixty-eight pages, numbered and initialed by Mr. Buchet, principal writer and judge." (Signed) Buchet. And in the Baptismal register of the chapel of St. Joseph, at Prairie du Rocher, appears an entry which has a strangely familiar sound. For it recites that several persons, adults and children, were baptized together, in the "presence of their parents, brothers, uncles, mutual friends, their sisters, their cousins, and their aunts." This, palpably, is the germ of "Pinafore," which Illinois may therefore take the credit of originating, long before our era!

New Chartres, and the other villages in the neighborhood, and the Fort, rested secure in the belief that, although Canada had surrendered, Louisiana, with the Illinois country, would still be preserved by the King, who might thence reconquer his lost possessions. Hence, like a thunder-clap, came the news that on the 10th of Feb., 1763, Louis XV. had ratified the treaty transferring them to the British Government. The aged Bienville, then living in Paris, with tears in his eyes, begged that the colony, to which he had given the best years of his life, might be spared to France, but in vain. With a stroke of his pen, the weak King ceded to Great Britain the Canadas, the Illinois, and all the valley of the Mississippi east of the river. While at Fort Chartres they were in daily expectation of news of the coming of British troops to take possession, an expedition arrived from New Orleans to settle at the Illinois. It was headed by Pierre Laclede, the representative of a company of merchants engaged in the fur trade. Learning here of the treaty of cession, he at once decided to establish a new post in the territory, west of the Mississippi, supposed to be still French ground. Neyon de Villiers permitted him to store his goods and quarter his company at the Fort, and Laclede, after an exploring tour, selected a fine bluff, sixty miles to the northward, for the site of his colony. He foresaw something of its future importance, and, returning to Fort Chartres for the winter, discoursed with enthusiasm upon its prospects, and took possession in the spring. This was the beginning of the city of St. Louis. Many of the French from the Illinois followed him, even transporting their houses to the other shcre, so great was their desire to live under their own flag. And terrible was their disappointment, when the secret treaty with Spain was made known, by which their faithless King ceded all his dominions beyond the Mississippi to the nation which had so long disputed with France her foothold there. Their last estate seemed worse than their first, for much as they detested the defiant banner of Britain, with a deeper hatred they regarded the gloomy ensign of Spain. Many more of the unhappy colonists descended the Mississippi, with Neyon de Villiers, in the belief that lower Louisiana was to remain under French control, and that their condition would be bettered there, only to be bitterly disappointed. Those who remained felt their hopes revive, as time passed on and the red-coats came not.

The veteran St. Ange, who had returned from Vincennes to play the last sad act of the drama, with a little garrison of forty men, still held the Fort, although it was the only place in North America at which the white flag of the Bourbons was flying. All else had been ceded and surrendered, but the way to the west was not yet open, for Pontiac was a lion in the path. The British victory was not complete until that flag was lowered, and repeated efforts to accomplish this were made. Again and again were they thwarted by the Forest Chieftain. Major Loftus, ascending the Mississippi with a force to take possession of Fort Chartres, was greeted with a volley at the bluffs, still called Loftus Heights, and retreated to Pensacola. Captain Pitman, seeking to find his way from Mobile in the guise of a trader, gave up the attempt as too hazardous. Captain Morris, sent from Detroit to arrange for the surrender of the Fort, was met by Pontiac, who, squatting in front of him, opened the interview by observing that the British were liars, and asked if he had come to lie to them like the rest. Attentions much less courteous were received from individuals of the Kickapoo persuasion, and Morris turned back, while still several hundred miles from his destination. Lieutenant Frazer, pushing down the Ohio, reached Kaskaskia, where he fell into Pontiac's hands, who kept him all one night in dread of being boiled alive, and at daybreak shipped him to New Orleans by canoe express, with the cheerful information that the kettle was boiling over a large fire to receive any other Englishmen who came that way. Frazer could only console himself, for his other-wise fruitless voyage down both the Ohio and the Mississippi, with the thought that he had been nearer to the objective point than any other officer, and had seen a great deal of the country. George Croghan, Sir William Johnson's interpreter, following Frazer on the same errand, was waylaid by the Shawnees on the Ohio and sent to the Indian villages on the Wabash, whence he took Morris' route to Detroit. The French and Spanish officers in Louisana, laughed at the British failures to reach a fort they claimed to own, and suggested that an import-ant party had been omitted in the treaty of cession, and that a new one should be made with King Pontiac. Meanwhile that sovereign was ordering into service some Illinois Indians, assembled near Fort Chartres, and when they showed a reluctance to engage in hostilities against their new rulers, said to them: "Hesitate not, or I destroy you as fire does the prairie grass. Listen, and recollect these are the words of Pontiac!" Their scruples vanished with amazing rapidity, and they did his bidding. Then with his retinue of dusky warriors, he led the way through the tall gateway of Fort Chartres, and greeting St. Ange, as he sat in the government house, said "Father, I have long wished to see thee, to recall the battles which we fought together against the misguided Indians and the English dogs. I love the French, and I have come here with my warriors to avenge their wrongs." But St. Ange plainly told him that all was over; Onontio, their great French father could do no more for his red children; he was beyond the sea and could not hear their voices; and they must make peace with the English. Pontiac, at last convinced, gave up the contest, and made no opposition to the approach from Fort Pitt, by the Ohio, of a detachment of the 42d High-landers, the famous Black Watch, under Captain Sterling, to whom St. Ange formally surrendered the Fort on the 10th of October, 1765. The lilies of France gave place to the red cross of St. George, and the long struggle was ended. At Fort Chartres the great empire of France in the New World ceased forever.

The minute of the surrender of Fort Chartres to M. Sterling, appointed by M. de Gage, Governor of New York, Commander of His Britannic Majesty's troops in North America, is preserved in the French archives at Paris. The Fort is carefully described in it, with its arched gateway, fifteen feet high; a cut-stone platform above the gate, with a stair of nineteen stone steps, having a stone balustrade, leading to it; its walls of stone eighteen feet in height; and its four bastions, each with forty-eight loop-holes, eight embrasures, and a sentry-box, the whole in cut stone. And within, the great store-house, ninety feet long by thirty wide, two stories high, and gable-roofed; the guard-house having two rooms above for the chapel and missionary quarters; the government-house 84 x 32, with iron gates and a stone porch, a coach-house and pigeon-house adjoining, and a large stone well inside; the intendant's house of stone and iron, with a portico; the two rows of barracks, each 128 feet long; the magazine thirty-five feet wide, thirty-eight feet long, and thirteen feet high above the ground, with a doorway of cut stone, and two doors, one of wood and one of iron; the bake-house with two ovens, and a stone well in front; the prison with four cells of cut stone, and iron doors; and one large relief gate to the north; the whole enclosing an area of more than four acres. The English had insisted that, under the treaty of cession, the guns in all the forts belonged to them. The French Governor, of Louisiana, disputed the claim, but consented to leave those at the Illinois, with a promise of their restoration, if his view proved correct. Hence the cannon of Fort Chartres were transferred with it, for the time at least.

St. Ange and his men took boat for St. Louis, where, feeling that their sovereign had utterly deserted them, they soon decided to exchange the service of his Most Christian Majesty of France, for that of his Most Catholic Majesty of Spain. They were speedily enrolled in the garrison of St. Louis, of which St. Ange was appointed to the command, to the great satisfaction of his comrades and his old neighbors from the Illinois. One tragedy signalized the accession of the new government at Fort Chartres. Two young officers, one French and the other English, were rival suitors for the hand of a young lady in the neighborhood, and a quarrel arose which led to a duel. They fought with small-swords early on a Sunday morning, near the Fort, the Englishman was slain, and the Frenchman made haste to descend the river to New Orleans. The story of this, no doubt the first duel fought in Illinois, was related, nearly forty years after its occurrence, by an aged Frenchman, who was an eye-witness of the combat, to the chronicler who has preserved the account. With the departure of the French soldiers, the last spark of life in the village of New Chartres went out. On the register, then in use in the church of St. Anne, was written, "The above-mentioned church (parochial of St. Anne of New Chartres) having been abolished, the rest of the paper which was in this book has been taken for the service of the church at Kaskaskia." And the Mississippi, as if bent upon destroying every vestige of the once happy and prosperous village, encroached upon its site until a large portion of it was swept away. Shortly after its abandonment, the parish register of Prairie du Rocher, which place continued to be occupied by the French, records the removal of the bodies of the Reverend Fathers Gagnon and Collet, priests of St. Anne of New Chartres, from the ruined cemetery near that church on the point in the river, and their burial in the chapel of St. Joseph, at Prairie du Rocher.

The Illinois had now become an British colony, "in the days when George the Third was King." The simple French inhabitants with difficulty accustomed themselves to the change, and longed for the paternal sway of the commanders of their own race. It is said that soon after the British occupation, the officer, in authority at Fort Chartres, died suddenly, and there being no one competent to succeed him, the wheels of government stopped. And that St. Ange, hearing, at St. Louis, of the confusion in his old province, repaired to Fort Chartres, restored order, and remained there until another British officer could reach the spot. The story is typical of the man, who deserves a wider fame than he has won. For he was a fine exemplar of the fidelity, the courage, and the true gentleness, which are worthy of the highest honor. He spent a long life in the arduous duties of a frontier officer, commanding escorts through the wilderness, stationed at the different posts in the North-West in turn, and for more than fifty years associated with the Illinois country, which became the home of his family. Born in Canada, and entering the French army as a boy, he grew gray in the service, and when surrendered to the foeman, he had so long opposed, by the unworthy King, who made no provision for the men who had stood so steadfastly for him, he was more faithful to France than Louis XV. had been. For his removal to St. Louis, and acceptance of a Spanish commission, were in the interest and for the protection of his misled countrymen, who had settled at that place solely that they might still be French subjects. There he remained, the patriarch of the infant settlement, beloved and honored by all, until his death, at the age of seventy-six, in the year of the commencement of our revolution. And all who knew him, friends and foes, countrymen and foreigners, white men and red, alike bear testimony to the uprightness, the steady fortitude, the unshrinking courage, the kindliness and nobility of Louis St. Ange de Belle Rive, the last French Commandant of the Illinois.

In December of the year of the surrender, Major Farmer, with a strong detachment of the 34th British Foot, arrived at the Fort from Mobile, and took command. The following year he was relieved by Colonel Edward Cole, a native of Rhode Island, an officer in the Old French War, who comanded a regiment under General Wolfe at the siege of Quebec, and was at the capture of Havana by the Earl of Albemarle. In letters written from the Fort, in 1766 to 1768, to his old comrade and partner in busi- ness, Colonel Henry Van Schaick, he says, "This country is far from answering my expectations in any other point than the soil. I have enjoyed but a small share of health since I arrived. I have been much deceived in the description of this country, and am determined to quit it as soon as I can. No comfort. Indians eternally about me." During his term of office, Captain Philip Pitman, a British engineer officer, the same who had unsuccess- fully endeavored to reach the Illinois during Pontiac's rule, visited the Fort in pursuance of his orders to examine the British posts in the Mississippi Valley. In his report he says: "The walls of Fort Chartres are two feet two inches thick, and the entrance is through a very handsome gate." He describes the works and buildings very fully, and concludes as follows: "It is generally believed that this is the most convenient and best built Fort in North America." In 1768, Col. Cole was followed by a Col. Reed, who became so notorious for his oppression of the people, that he was speedily relieved by John Wilkins, Lieut.- Colonel of the 18th or Royal Irish, the former commander of Fort Niagara, who reached the Illinois, with seven companies of his regiment, from Philadelphia, by way of Pittsburg, in Sept., 1768. From the correspondence of Ensign George Butricke, an officer in this expedition, we learn that, on their way down the Ohio, they killed so many buffalo that they commonly served out one a day to each company, and they were forty-three days on the way, from Pittsburg to Kaskaskia. Speaking of Fort Chartres as "built of stone, with bastions at each angle, and very good barracks of stone," he describes the land around it as the finest in the known world, and gives his opinion to the effect that "it is a shocking unhealthy country." Col. Wilkins, under a proclamation from General Gage, established a court of law, with seven judges, to sit at Fort Chartres, and administer the law of England, the first court of common-law jurisdiction, west of the Alleghanies. The old French court of the royal jurisdiction of the Illinois, with its single judge, governed by the civil law, had ceased with the surrender. Its records for many years were preserved at Kaskaskia, where the late Judge Breese saw and made extracts from them. When the county-seat was removed, less care was taken of them, and within a few years past, these documents, so interesting and valuable to the antiquarian and the historian, have been used by veritable Illinois Vandals to light the fires in a country court-house, and but a solitary fragment now remains. In Wilkins' time, that famous warrior, Pontiac, was basely slain at Cahokia, by an Illinois Indian. St. Ange, then commanding at St. Louis, honoring the noble red man, whom he had known long and well, brought the body to his fort, and gave it solemn burial. The friends of Pontiac, avenging his death, pursued one fragment of the Illinois tribe to the walls of Fort Chartres, and slew many there, the British refusing them admission. At Prairie du Rocher, about this period, is recorded the marriage of a French soldier, of the garrison of St. Louis, with the written permission of M. de St. Ange, his commander, to an Englishwoman from Salisbury, in Wiltshire, which the good priest writes, "Solbary, in the province of Wuilser." It is significant of the different races, and the varying sovereignties in that portion of our country, that a French soldier, from the Spanish city of St. Louis, should be married to an Englishwoman by a French priest, in the British colony of Illinois.

The occupation of Fort Chartres, however, by the soldiers of any nation, was drawing to a close. For seven years only the British ruled there, though, doubtless, believing it to be their permanent headquarters for the whole North-West. But the Mississippi had ever been a French river, and could not bide the presence of the rival nation on its banks. Its waters murmured the names of Marquette and Joliet, of LaSalle and Tonti, and their memories would not suffer it to rest contented with successors of another race. So it rose in its might and assailed the Fort, and on a stormy night in spring-time its resistless flood tore away a bastion, and a part of the river wall. The British in all haste fled across the submerged meadows, taking refuge on the hills above Kaskaskia; and from the year 1772, Fort Chartres was never occupied again.

The capricious Mississippi, as if satisfied with this recognition of its power, now devoted itself to the reparation of the damage it had wrought. The channel between the Fort and the island in front of it, once forty feet deep, began to fill up, and, ultimately, the main shore and the island were united, leaving the Fort a mile or more inland. A thick growth of trees speedily concealed it from the view of those passing upon the river, and the high road from Cahokia to Kaskaskia, which at first ran between the Fort and the river, was soon after located at the foot of the bluffs, three miles to the eastward. These changes, which left the Fort completely isolated and hidden, together with the accounts of the British evacuation, gave rise to the reports of its total distruction by the river. Parkman, alluding to it as it was in 1764, says, "The encroaching Mississippi was destined before many years to engulf curtain and bastion in its ravenous abyss." A work relating to the history of the North-West, published only last year, informs us that "the spot on which Fort Chartres stood became the channel of the river," and even some who have lived for years in its neighborhood will tell you that it is entirely swept away. But this is entirely erroneous; the ruins still remain; and had man treated it as kindly as the elements, the old Fort would be nearly perfect to-day.

After the British departed, an occasional band of Indians found shelter for a little time in the lonely buildings, but otherwise, the solitude which claimed for its own the once busy fortress, remained unbroken for many a year to come. Congress, in 1788, reserved to our government a tract of land one mile square, on the Mississippi, extending as far above as below Fort Chartres, including the said Fort, the buildings, and improvements adjoining the same. It would have been well to provide for the preservation of this monument of the romantic era of our history, but, of course, nothing of the sort was done. The enactment simply prevented any settlement upon the reservation, and left the Fort to become more and more a part of the wilderness, and its structures a prey to the spoiler. Now and then an adventurous traveler found his way thither. Quaint old Gov. Reynolds, who saw it in 1802, says, "It is an object of antiquarian curiosity. The trees, undergrowth, and brush are mixed and interwoven with the old walls. It presented the most striking contrast between a savage wilderness, filled with wild beasts and reptiles, and the remains of one of the largest and strongest fortifications on the continent. Large trees were growing in the houses which once contained the elegant and accomplished French officers and soldiers." And then, with a hazy idea of rivalling the prophecy of the lion and the lamb, he adds, "Cannon, snakes, and bats were sleeping together in peace in and around this fort." Major Amos Stoddard, of the U.S. Engineers, who took possession of Upper Louisiana for our government under the treaty of cession, in 1804, visited Fort Chartres and thus describes it, "Its figure is quadrilateral with four bastions, the whole of lime-stone, well cemented. The walls are still entire. A spacious square of barracks and a capacious magazine are in good preservation. The enclosure is covered with trees from seven to twelve inches in diameter. In fine this work exhibits a splendid ruin. The inhabitants have taken away great quantities of material to adorn their own buildings." Brackenridge, U.S. Judge for the District of Louisiana, in a work published in 1817, has this passage, "Fort de Chartres is a noble ruin, and is visited by strangers as a great curiosity. I was one of a party of ladies and gentlemen who ascended in a barge from Ste. Genevieve, nine miles below. The outward wall, barracks, and magazine are still standing. There are a number of cannon lying half buried in the earth with their trunnions broken off. In visiting the various parts, we started a flock of wild turkeys, which had concealed themselves in this hiding-place. I remarked a kind of enclosure near, which, according to tradition, was fitted up by the officers as a kind of arbor where they could sit and converse in the heat of the day." In 1820, Beck, the publisher of a Gazeteer of Illinois and Missouri, made a careful survey of the remains of the Fort. He speaks of it then as a splendid ruin, "the walls in some places perfect, the buildings in ruins, except the magazine, and in the hall of one of the houses an oak growing, eighteen inches in diameter." Hall, the author of a book entitled Romance of the West, was at Fort Chartres, in 1829. "Although the spot was familiar to my companion," he says, "it was with some difficulty that we found the ruins, which are covered with a vigorous growth of forest trees and a dense undergrowth of bushes and vines. Even the crumbling pile itself is thus overgrown, the tall trees rearing their stems from piles of stone, and the vines creeping over the tottering walls. The buildings were all razed to the ground, but the lines of the foundations could be easily traced. A large vaulted powder-magazine remained in good preservation. The exterior wall was thrown down in some places, but in others retained something like its original height and form. And it was curious to see in the gloom of a wild forest these remnants of the architecture of a past age." The Fort Chartres Reservation was opened to entry in 1849, no provision being made concerning what remained of the Fort. The land was taken up by settlers, the area of the works cleared of trees, and a cabin built within it, and the process of demolition hastened by the increasing number of those who resorted there for building material. Governor Reynolds

PLAN OF FORT CHARTRES
ON THE MISSISSIPPI.

Drawn from a survey made by N. Hansen, Esq., of Illinois, and L. C. Beck, in 1820.

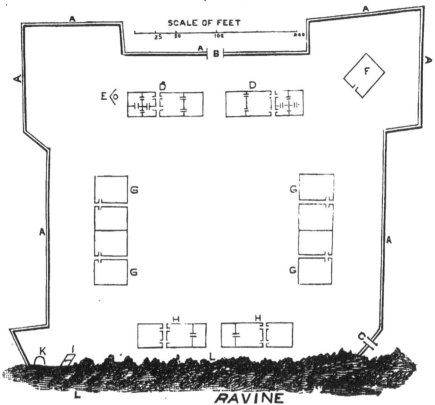

A A A   The exterior wall—1447 feet.

B   The gate or entrance to the fort.

C   A small gate.

D D   The two houses formerly occupied by the commandant and commissary, each 96 feet in length and 30 in breadth.

E   The well.

F   The magazine.

G G G G   Houses formerly occupied as barracks, 135 feet in length, 36 in breadth.

H H   Formerly occupied as a storehouse and guard-house, 90 feet by 24.

I   The remains of small magazine.

K   The remains of a furnace.

L L L   A ravine, which in the spring is filled with water.   Between this and the river, which is about half-a-mile, is a thick growth of cotton wood.

The area of the fort is about four square acres.

came again in 1854, and found "Fort Chartres a pile of mouldering ruins, and the walls torn away almost even with the surface."

To one visiting the site but a year ago, the excursion afforded
as strong a contrast between the past and the present as may
readily be found. Leaving the railway at the nearest point to
the ruins, the brisk new town of Red Bud, twenty miles distant,
the greater part of the drive over the prairie and through the
forest which intervene, is as monotonous as a ride anywhere in
Illinois may properly be. But when you reach the bluff, far
overlooking the lordly Mississippi, and its lowlands to the
Missouri hills beyond, and wind down the road cut deeply into
its face to the little village of Prairie du Rocher, lying at its foot,
a change comes over the scene. The wide and shaded village
streets with the French names above the little stores, the houses
built as in Canada, with dormer-windows and piazzas facing to
the south, the mill bearing the name the Jesuits gave the site, the
foreign accent and appearance of the people, the very atmosphere,
so full of rest and quiet, to which hurry is unknown, all combine
to make one feel as if in another time and another land than
ours. It is as though a little piece of old France had been
transplanted to the Mississippi, a century since, and forgotten; or
as if a stratum of the early French settlements at the Illinois, a
hundred years ago or more, had sunk down below the reach of
time and change, with its ways and customs and people intact,
and still pursued its former life unmindful of the busy nineteenth
century on the uplands above its head. It was not surprising to
be told that at the house of the village priest some ancient relics
were to be seen, and that some ancient documents had once
been there. In such a place such things should always be. But
it was a surprise, when shown into a room adorned with portraits
of Pius IX. and Leo XIII., and expecting to see a venerable
man with black robes, and, perhaps, the tonsure, to be suddenly
greeted by a joyous youth, in German student costume, with a
mighty meerschaum in his hand, who introduced himself as the
priest in charge of the parish of St. Joseph of Prairie du Rocher.
Arrived but six months before from the old country, he had been
stationed here because of his knowledge of French, which is
spoken by nearly all of the 250 families in the parish, including a
number of colored people, the descendants of the slaves of the
early settlers. He led the way to his sanctum, where he displayed, with pride, three chalices and a monstrance, or receptacle
for the wafer, very old and of quaint workmanship, made of solid
silver, and a tabernacle of inlaid wood, all supposed to have
belonged to the church of St. Anne of Fort Chartres. He had

also a solid silver table-castor, marked 1680, the property of his parish, the history of which is unknown.   At an inquiry for old manuscripts, he produced, from a lumber-room, a bundle of dis-colored papers, fast going to decay, which he had found in the house when he took possession, but of which he knew but little. Almost the first inspection revealed a marriage register of the church of St. Anne, with the autographs of Makarty and De Villiers, and subsequent examination showed that these papers comprised a large part of the registers of that parish, as well as the early records of St. Joseph of Prairie du Rocher.

Such an experience was a fitting prelude to the sight of the old Fort itself, though this was, indeed, difficult to find.   In the early day all roads in the Illinois country led to Fort Chartres. Highways thither are the most prominent feature of the old village plats and ancient maps of the region.   Now, not even a path leads to it.   The simple French people along the way could not believe that any one could really wish to visit the old Fort, and with kindly earnestness insisted that the intended destination must be the river landing, which takes its name from the Fort, but is some miles away from it.   By dint of repeated inquiries, a course was found which led to the goal after a five-mile drive from Prairie du Rocher.   The ruins were approached by a farm-road across a beautiful level field, green with winter wheat, and the first sight of the low bank, which marks the position of the walls, and of the old magazine standing bravely up against the forest background, was a sufficient reward for the journey.   En-tering the enclosure through a rude farm-gate, which stands just in the place of its lofty predecessor of carved stone, the line of the walls and the corner bastions can be readily traced by the mounds of earth covered with scattered fragments of stone, beneath which, doubtless, the heavy foundations remain, except at the corner swept away by the river.   On two sides the outline of the ditch can be seen, and the cellars of the commandant's and intendant's houses, and of the barracks, are plainly visible, half filled with débris, under which, perhaps, the old cannon of Louis XIV. are still lying.   Time has settled the question of title to them, and they belong neither to France nor Britain now.   One angle of the main wall remains, and is utilized as the substructure of a stable.   Two rude houses, occupied by farm tenants, are within the enclosure, which has been cleared of trees, save a few tall ones near the magazine and alongside the ditch. In front, the ground is open and under cultivation, and, looking from the old gateway, you have before you the prospect which must often have pleased the eyes of the officers of France and

Britain, gazing from the cut-stone platform above the arch; the little knoll in front where Boisbriant's land-grant to himself commenced, the level plateau dotted with clumps of forest trees, the gleam of the little lake in the lowland and beyond, the beautiful buttresses of rock, rounded and shaped as if by the hand of man, supporting the upland which bounds the view. Of the vanished village of St. Anne, scarcely a vestige remains, save a few garden-plants growing wild on the plain. Occasionally a well belonging to one of its houses is found, but there is no sign of the church, where "sales were made in a high and audible voice, while the people went in and out in great numbers." The site of St. Philip is covered by a farm, but to this day a part of its long line of fields is known as "the King's Highway," though there is no road there, and it is supposed that this was the route along which Renault brought the supplies from his grant to the river for transfer to his mines.

Yet, though so much has gone of the ancient surroundings and of the Fort itself, it was an exceeding pleasure to find the old magazine, still almost complete, and bearing itself as sturdily as if conscious that it alone is left of all the vast domain of France in America, and resolute to preserve its memory for the ages to come. It stands within the area of the south-eastern bastion, solidly built of stone, its walls four feet in thickness, sloping upward to perhaps twelve feet from the ground, and rounded at the top. It is partially covered with vines and moss, and one might travel far and wide in our land to find an object so picturesque and so venerable. But for the loss of its iron doors, and the cut stone about the doorway, it is well-nigh as perfect as the day it was built. Within, a few steps lead to the solid stone floor, some feet below the surface, and the interior, nearly thirty feet square, is entirely uninjured. You may note the arched stone roof, the careful construction of the heavy walls, and the few small apertures for light and air, curiously protected against injury from without. Here one may invoke the shades of Makarty, and De Villiers, and St. Ange, and easily bring back the past. For, as it is to-day, it has seen them all, as they went to and fro before it, or examined its store of shot and shell; it has heard the word of command as the grenadiers drilled on the parade-ground hard by; it has watched the tawny chieftains and their followers trooping in single file through the adjacent gateway; and past its moss-grown walls the bridal processions of Madeleine Loisel and Elizabeth Montcharveaux, and the other fair ladies from the Fort, have gone to the little church of St. Anne. And gazing at it in such a mood, until all about was peopled with "the airy shapes of long ago," and one beheld again the gallant company which laid the foundations of this fortress with such high hope and purpose, the hurrying scouts passing through its portals with tidings of Indian foray or Spanish march, the valiant leaders setting forth from its walls on distant expeditions against savage or civilized foe, the colonists flocking to its store-house or council-chamber, the dusky warriors throng-ing its enclosure with Chicago or Pontiac at their head, the gathering there of those who founded a great city, the happy village at its gates, and the scenes of its momentous surrender, which sealed the loss of an empire to France; it seemed not unreasonable to wish that the State of Illinois might, while yet there is time, take measures to permanently preserve, for the sake of the memories, the romance, and the history interwoven in its fabric, what still remains of Old Fort Chartres.

COL. JOHN TODD'S RECORD-BOOK.

THE early records of "the Illinois," as the region including our State was formerly called, unfortunately, have not been preserved. Those of its civil and judicial administration, during the sixty years of its organized government as a royal province, and the subsequent period of its existence as a county of Virginia, would be of exceeding value to him who shall properly write the history of Illinois. A large collection of such papers remained at Kaskaskia, once the capital, successively, of province, territory, and state, until the day came when the ancient village was obliged to yield even the honor of being a county-seat to the neighboring city of Chester. To the latter place, several boxes filled with these papers were then removed, and stood for years in the hall of its court-house, until, by neglect or wanton misuse, their contents were lost or destroyed. One, however, of these mementos of the past, and not the least in worth among them, was recently found in an office of this court-house, in a receptacle for fuel, just in time to save it from the fiery fate of many of its companions, and is now in the custody of the Chicago Historical Society. This is the original Record or Minute-Book of Colonel John Todd, the first civil governor of the Illinois country.

When George Rogers Clark had captured the British posts beyond the Ohio, under the authority of Virginia, that State was quick to act for the preservation of the rights thus acquired. Kaskaskia was taken on the 4th of July, 1778; the first surrender of Vincennes, or St. Vincent, as it was sometimes called, occurred soon after; and in October, of the same year, the General Assembly of Virginia passed "An Act for establishing the County of Illinois, and for the more effectual protection and defence thereof." The young Commonwealth, only in the third year of its own independent existence, and then with the other revolted colonies, engaged in a death-struggle with the Mother Country, did not shrink from the duty of providing a suitable

4

government for the immense territory thus added to its domain. The Act recites the successful expedition of the Virginia militia-men in the country adjacent to the Mississippi, and that good faith and safety require that the citizens thereof, who have acknowledged the Commonwealth, shall be supported and pro-tected, and that some temporary form of government, adapted to their circumstances, shall be established. It provides that all the citizens of Virginia, settled on the western side of the Ohio, shall be included in a distinct county, to be called Illinois County. The vast area, afterwards ceded to the United States under the name of the North-West Territory, and now divided into five States, then composed a single county of Virginia. Of this county the governor of the State was authorized to appoint a county-lieutenant, or commandant, who could appoint and com-mission deputy-commandants, militia-officers, and commissaries. The religion and customs of the inhabitants were to be respected, and all civil officers were to be chosen by a majority of the inhabitants of the respective districts. The County-Lieutenant had power to pardon all offenders, except murder and treason. The Governor was authorized to levy five hundred men to garri-son and protect the county, and keep up communications with Virginia, and with the Spanish settlements, and to take measures to supply goods to the inhabitants and friendly Indians. Such was the first Bill of Rights of Illinois.

The Governor of the State of Virginia, upon whom devolved the duty of selecting the commandant of the country of Illinois, was the first who ever held that office, the immortal patriot, Patrick Henry; and the man whom he chose for this difficult and responsible position was John Todd. He was not unknown on the frontier nor at the capital. Born in Pennsylvania, and educated in Virginia, he had practised law in the latter colony for several years, when, in 1775, he removed to the Kentucky country. He was one of those who met at Boonesboro', in the spring of that year, under the great elm tree, near the fort, to establish the proprietary government of the so-called colony of Transylvania, comprising more than half of the modern State of of Kentucky, and he was very prominent in the counsels of its House of Delegates or Representatives, the first legislative body organized west of the Alleghanies. He preëmpted large tracts of land near the present city of Lexington, and is said to have been one of the band of pioneers, who, while encamped on its site, heard of the opening battle of the Revolution in the far East, and named their infant settlement in its honor. When the agents of the Kentucky settlers had obtained a gift of powder from Virginia.

for the defence of the frontier, in the following year, and had brought it down the Ohio to the Three Islands, Todd led a small party through the forests to transport it to one of the forts, but was beaten back, after a bloody contest with the Indians. Early in 1777, the first court in Kentucky opened its sessions àt Harrisburg, and he was one of the justices. Shortly after, he was chosen one of the representatives of Kentucky in the legislature of Virginia, and went to the capital to fulfil this duty. The following year he accompanied George Rogers Clarke in his expedition to the Illinois, and was the first man to enter Fort Gage, at Kaskaskia, when it was taken from the British, and was present at the final capture of Vincennes.

Meanwhile the Act, above mentioned, had been passed, and the Governor had no difficulty in deciding whom to appoint County-Lieutenant of Illinois. At Williamsburg, then the capital of the Old Dominion, in the former mansion of the royal rulers of the whilom colony, Patrick Henry, on the 12th of December, 1778, indited his letter of appointment to John Todd, Esq., and entered it in the very book now·before us. It occupies the first five pages, and probably is in Patrick Henry's handwriting. At all events his own signature is subscribed thereto. This letter is not such a one as territorial governors would be likely to receive in these later days. It deals with higher things than those which occupy the modern politician. The opening paragraph informs John Todd, Esq., that by virtue of the Act of the General Assembly, which establishes the County of Illinois, he is appointed County-Lieutenant, or Commandant, there, and refers him to the law for the general tenor of his conduct. It continues as follows: "The grand objects which are disclosed. to the view of your countrymen will prove beneficial, or otherwise, according to the value and abilities of those who are called to direct the affairs of that remote country. The present crisis, rendered favorable by the good disposition of the French and Indians, may be improved to great purposes, but if, unhappily, it should be lost, a return of the same attachments to us may never happen. Considering, therefore, that early prejudices are so hard to wear out, you will take care to cultivate and conciliate the affections of the French and Indians." * * * "Although great reliance is placed on your prudence in managing the people you are to reside among, yet considering you as unacquainted in some degree with their genius, usages, and manners, as well as the geography of the country, I recommend it to you to consult and advise with the most intelligent and upright persons who may fall in your way."

His relations to the military, under Col. Clark, are next considered; the necessity of coöperation with and aid to them, in defence against, or attack upon, hostile British and Indians, summing up with the general direction, to consider himself "at the head of the civil department, and as such, having the command of the militia who are not to be under the command of the military, until ordered out by the civil authority, and to act in conjunction with them." He is advised "on all occasions to inculcate on the people the value of liberty, and the difference between the state of free citizens of this Commonwealth, and that of slavery, to which the Illinois was destined, and that they are to have a free and equal representation, and an improved jurisprudence." His care must be to remove "the grievances that obstruct the happiness, increase, and prosperity of that country, and his constant attention to see that the inhabitants have justice administered." He is to discountenance and punish every attempt to violate the property of the Indians, particularly in their land.. To the Spanish commandant, near Kaskaskia, he is to tender friendship and services, and cultivate the strictest connection with him and his people, and a letter to him, from Governor Henry, Todd is to deliver in person. And he is warned that the matters given him in charge "are singular in their nature and weighty in their consequences to the people immediately concerned, and to the whole State. They require the fullest exertion of ability and unwearied diligence." Then with that high sense of justice and humanity which distinguished the man, Henry turns from State affairs to right the wrongs of the helpless wife and children of his country's enemy. The family of Mr. Rocheblave, the late British commandant at Kaskaskia, had been left among the hostile people there, while the husband and father was a prisoner in Virginia, and their possessions had been confiscated. Todd is informed "that they must not suffer for want of that property of which they had been bereft by our troops; it is to be restored to them, if possible; if this can not be done, the public must support them." And the letter concludes with a direction to send an express once in three months, bringing a general account of affairs, and with the mention of a contemplated plan for the appointment of an agent to supply the Illinois with goods on public account.

Conciliation of the newly enfranchised inhabitants, selection of competent advisers, defence against foreign and native enemies, subordination of the military to the civil arm of the government, establishment of Republican institutions, administration of equal justice to all, an alliance with friendly neighbors, encouragement of trade, and the exertion by the commandant of unwearied ability, diligence, and zeal, in behalf of his people; such are the principal heads of this able and, for its time, extraordinary State paper. It shows us that the man who had taken the grave responsibility of the secret instructions which led to the capture of the Illinois country, was competent to direct the next step in its career. He could wisely govern what had been bravely won. With all the cares of a new State engaged in a war for its independence resting upon his shoulders, proscribed as a traitor to the Mother Country, and writing almost within sound of the guns of the British fleet upon the James, he looked with calm vision into the future, and laid well the foundations of another Commonwealth beyond the Ohio.

This book, made precious by his pen, was entrusted to a faithful messenger, who carried it from tidewater across the mountains to Fort Pitt, thence down the Ohio, until he met with his destined recipient, and delivered to him his credentials. It is supposed, that Todd received it at Vincennes, then known to Virginians as St. Vincent, not long after the surrender of that place, on February 24th, 1779, and thereupon returned to the Kentucky country to make some necessary preparations for his new duties, and possibly to enlist some of the soldiers authorized to be raised by the Act under which he was appointed. At all events, he did not reach the Illinois country until the spring of 1779, as we learn from the journal of Colonel George Rogers Clark, who says, "The civil department in the Illinois had heretofore robbed me of too much of my time that ought to be spent in military reflection. I was now likely to be relieved by Col. John Todd, appointed by Government for that purpose. I was anxious for his arrival, and happy in his appointment, as the greatest intimacy and friendship subsisted between us; and on the —— day of May, (1779), had the pleasure of seeing him safely landed at Kaskaskias, to the joy of every person. I now saw myself happily rid of a piece of trouble that I had no delight in."

So came the new governor to his post, the bearer of Republican institutions to a land and a people but just freed from the rule of a foreign king. And with him he brought this very book containing in the memorable letter inscribed in its pages his own credentials, as well as the best evidence these new citizens could have that they were subjects no longer. This was no ordinary arrival at the goodly French village of Kaskaskia. In the eighty years of its existence, it had seen explorers and missionaries, priests and soldiers, famous travelers and men of high degree, come and go, but never before one sent to administer the laws of a peoples' government for the benefit of the governed. We may imagine its inhabitants gathered at the river side to watch the slow approach of a heavy boat, flying a flag still strange to them, as it toils against the current to the end of its long voyage down the Ohio and up the Mississippi. And when there lands from it one with the mien of authority, (having, perchance, this book under his arm), they are ready to render him the homage exacted by royal governors, and here and there a voice even cries, "Vive le Roi." And, as they are reminded that they are under a free government now, and learn that the new comer is their own County-Lieutenant, on their way back to the village, we may hear Francois and Baptiste say to one another, "Who is it that rules over us now?" and, "What is this free government of which they speak?" "Is it a good thing, think you?" Small blame to them if their wits were puzzled. Less than fourteen years before they had been loyal liegemen to King Louis of France; then came a detachment of kilted Highlanders and presto! they were under the sway of King George of Great Britain; a few years passed, and one July morning, a band with long beards and rifles looked down from the heights of Fort Gage and raised a new banner over them, and now there was yet another arrival, which, though seemingly peaceful, might mean more than appeared. Perhaps the very last solution of the mystery which occurred to them, was that thenceforth they were to take part in their own government.

Whether Todd regarded his department as such "a piece of trouble," as Clark found it, we have no means of knowing, but certainly he addressed himself at once to his work. Under the clause of the statute which authorized him to appoint and commission deputy-commandants and militia-officers, he took action, probably as soon as he arrived, and recorded it in his book. At page 6 is the first entry in Todd's handwriting, which reads as follows:

"Made out the military commissions for the District of Kaskaskia, dated May 14th, 1779:

RICHARD WINSTON, Commandant, as Capt.
NICHOLAS JANIS, First Co. Capt.
BAPTISTE CHARLEVILLE, 1 Lieut.
CHARLES CHARLEVILLE, 2 Lieut.
MICHAEL GODIS, Ensign.
JOSEPH DUPLASSY, 2d Capt.
NICHOLAS LE CHANIE, 1 Lieut.
CHARLES DANEE, 2 Lieut.
BATISTE JANIS, Ensign."

"17th May, sent a Com. of Command of Prairie du Rocher, and Capt. of the Militia to Jean B. Barbeau.

The District of Kohokia:

FRANCOIS TROTTER, Comnd't.

TOURANGEAU, Capt. 1.

BEAULIEU, Capt. 2.

GURADIN, Lieut.

P. MARTHIR, Lieut.

SANFARON, Ensign.

Comns dated 14th May, 1779, 3d year of the Commonwealth."

This was the earliest organization of a militia force proper, in this region, and these officers were the first of the long line, adorned by many brilliant names, of those who have held Illinois commissions. There was significance, too, in the concluding of this entry with the words, "Third year of the Commonwealth." It meant that in this "remote country," as Patrick Henry called it, men felt the change from subjects to freemen then being wrought by the great Revolution, and that they were playing a part in it.

And this is emphasized in the succeeding minute.

Todd appears to have next put in force the statutory provision that all civil officers were to be chosen by a majority of the citizens in each district, and on pages 7 and 8 he records the "List of the Court of Kaskaskia, the Court of Kohokias, and the Court of St. Vincennes," and adds, "*as elected by the people.*" As elected by the people, and not as appointed by a king—as chosen by the citizens of each district, and not by the whim of some royal minister, thousands of miles away, across the sea. This was indeed a change. For more than half a century the the settlements at the Illinois had known a court and a judge. But the laws, and the administrators thereof, had been imported from a distant kingdom, and with the framing of the one or the selection of the other, they had had nothing whatever to do. And, without doubt, the election here recorded was their first exercise of the rights of citizens of a republic, and the first exercise of such rights within the territory of Illinois. In these lists appear a number of names of more or less note in the old time, and some of those already recited in the militia appointments. Richard Winston, Deputy-Commandant at Kaskaskia, filled also the office of Sheriff of that district, and Jean B. Barbeau found no inconsistency between his duties as Deputy-Commandant at Prairie du Rocher, and those of one of the judges of the court of his district. Nicholas Janis and Charles Charleville were also liable to be called from the Kaskaskia bench to do military duty, and at Cahokia, five of the seven judges held officers' commissions. This state of things may have been occasioned by the scarcity of men to take the new positions, so that "there were offices enough to go around" and to give some public-spirited citizens two apiece. If so, the modern office-seeker might well sigh for those good old times. An unusual circumstance appears in connection with the court of Vincennes. Against the name of one Cardinal, elected by the people as a judge, Todd has written "refused to serve." This is believed to be the only instance in our annals of a refusal to take an office. And it is feared that this unique individual left no descendants. No other of the name appears in any subsequent record of the territory, so far as known. It is possible that we ought to share the glory of this *rara avis* with the citizens of Indiana, since Vincennes is within the limits of that State. But, as he was at the time of this unexampled refusal a citizen of Illinois, we should strenuously claim him as one whose like will ne'er be seen again. After the list of the court of Vincennes, Todd notes his militia appointments at that place, the Chief-Justice P. Legras being also appointed Lieutenant-Colonel, and the first Associate-Justice, Major. Opposite two of the names is written, "rank not settled," as if already that jealousy, which is the bane of the profession of arms, had sprung up. And a number of blanks are left, apparently to await the determination of that controversy, which seem never to have been filled.

Having organized the military and judicial departments of his government, the new commandant appears next to have given his attention to the encouragement of business. On page 11 of this book, appears a License for Trade, permitting "Richard M'Carthy, Gentleman, to traffick and merchandize, with all the liege subjects and Friends of the United States of America, of what nation soever they be, and to erect Factories and Stores at any convenient place or places he shall think proper within the Commonwealth." A careful proviso is made that "by virtue hereof no pretence shall be made to trespass upon the effects or property of individuals"; and the license is given under the hand and seal of John Todd, at Kaskaskia, the 5th June, 1779, in the 3rd year of the Commonwealth.

The financial question was the next to claim the attention of the busy County-Lieutenant, and he grappled with it sturdily. It was now the fourth year of the Revolutionary war, and the peculiar disadvantages of the continental currency, which had been severely felt at the East, began to be appreciated at the West as well. But John Todd did not hesitate to confront this evil, and, at any rate, devised a plan for its correction. Within a month of his arrival at Kaskaskia, on the 11th of June, 1779, he addressed a letter to the court of Kaskaskia, which appears on page 12 of his Record-Book. He informs it that "the only method America has to support the present just war is by her credit, which credit consists of her bills emitted from the different treasuries by which she engages to pay the bearer, at a certain time, gold and silver in exchange; that there is no friend to American Independence, who has any judgment, but soon expects to see it equal to gold and silver, but that merely from its uncommon quantity, and in proportion to it, arises the complaint of its want of credit. And one only remedy remains within his power, which is to receive, on behalf of government, such sums as the people shall be induced to lend upon a sure fund, and thereby decrease the quantity." He states that the mode of doing this is already planned, and requests the concurrence and assistance of the judges. His zeal for the cause led him slightly astray when he predicted that these bills would soon be equal to gold and silver, since, in the following year, continental money was worth just two cents on the dollar, and never became more valuable. But in other respects his scheme was not so erroneous. He did not indulge in the delusion that all troubles could be removed by an unlimited issue of paper money. On the contrary, he favored the retirement of a portion of that in circulation, and of a kind of redemption of the public promises to pay. On page 14 is set forth at length, "Plan for borrowing 33333⅓ dollars of Treasury notes, both belonging to this State and the United States." The preamble recites that owing to no other reason than the prodigious quantity of treasury notes, now in circulation, the value of almost every commodity has risen to most enormous prices, the preserving the credit of the said bills by reducing the quantity, requires some immediate remedy. And it is therefore declared that 21,000 acres of land, belonging to the Commonwealth, shall be laid off on the bank of the Mississippi in the district of Cahokia, 1000 acres to be reserved for a town, and the remainder to constitute a fund; and that the lender of money shall take a certificate for the sum, entitling him to demand, within two years, a title to his proportion of the land in said fund, or the sum originally advanced in gold and silver, with five per cent interest per annum. It is prudently provided that the State shall have the option of giving land or money, and to further protect a paternal government against any undue advantage being taken of it by its sons, notice is given that a deduction shall be made for all money hereafter discovered to be counterfeited. Then follow the commencement of a French translation of the plan, a copy of the instructions to the Commissioner for borrowing money upon this fund, which direct him to keep every man's money by itself, and the form of receipt to be issued. Henry H. Crutcher appears to have been appointed such Commissioner, and his bond, with George Slaughter and John Roberts as sureties to Mr. John Todd, Commander-in-Chief of the County of Illinois, in the penalty of $33,333⅓ for the safe keeping of the money, is next recorded under date of June 14th, 1779.

On the same date, this energetic "Commander-in-Chief" addresses himself to the subject of the land under his jurisdiction, and the title thereto. He issues a proclamation strictly enjoining all persons from making any new settlements on the flat lands within one league of the rivers Mississippi, Ohio, Illinois, and Wabash, except in the manner and form of settlements as heretofore made by the French inhabitants; and every inhabitant is required to lay before the persons appointed in each district for that purpose a memorandum of his or her land with their vouchers for the same. Warning is given that the number of adventurers who will soon run over this country, renders the above method necessary, as well as to ascertain the vacant land as to guard against trespasses which will be committed on land not of record. The object of this step evidently was not to discourage actual settlers, but to prevent the taking up of large, tracts of land by speculators; and it shows both wisdom and foresight on the part of the head of the Government.

The graver duties associated with that position were quickly to devolve upon John Todd, and on page 18 of his Record-Book is inscribed an entry, which reads very strangely at the present day. It is *verbatim* as follows:

"Illinois, to wit: To Richard Winston, Esq., Sheriff in chief of the District of Kaskaskia.

Negro Manuel, a Slave, in your custody, is condemned by the Court of Kaskaskia, after having made honorable Fine at the Door of the Church, to be chained to a post at the Water Side and there to be burnt alive and his ashes scattered, as appears to me by Record. This Sentence you are hereby required to put in execution on tuesday next at 9 o'clock in the morning, and this shall be your warrant. Given under my hand and seal at Kaskaskia the 13th day of June in the third year of the Commonwealth."

This is a grim record, and reveals a dark chapter in the early history of Illinois. It is not surprising that some one has drawn heavy lines across it as if to efface it forever. It is startling to reflect that barely one hundred years ago, within the territory now composing our State, a court of law deliberately sentenced a human being to be burned alive! It is possible that the attempted cancellation of the entry may mean that the warrant was revoked. And so let us hope for the sake of humanity. No other evidence, so far as known, of this peculiar case exists. But it is palpable that this inhuman penalty was actually fixed by the court, and as the statute deprived the commandant of the power to pardon in such cases, it is more probable that the sentence was actually executed. The cruel form of death, the color of the unfortunate victim, and the scattering of the ashes, all seem to indicate that this was one of the instances of the imagined crime of Voudouism or Negro Witchcraft, for which it is known that some persons suffered in the Illinois country about this time. Reynolds, in his Pioneer History, says, "In Cahokia about the year 1790, this superstition got the upperhand of reason, and several poor African slaves were immolated at the shrine of ignorance for this imaginary offence. An African negro, called Moreau, was hung for this crime on a tree not far southeast of Cahokia. It is stated that he had said he poisoned his master, but his mistress was too strong for his necromancy." There is no doubt that this is a correct statement of the facts, although the date of their occurrence is erroneously given. For on the next page of this Record-Book appears Todd's order for the detail of a guard for this very negro Moreau to the place of execution, dated June 15th, 1779, which, of course goes to show the probability of the infliction of the penalty above mentioned in the case of the negro, Manuel. This order in regard to Moreau, is as follows:

"To Capt. Nicholas Janis.

You are hereby required to call upon a party of your militia to guard Moreau, a slave condemned to execution, up to the town of Kohos. Put them under an officer. They shall be entitled pay rashtions and refreshment during the Time they shall be upon Duty to be certifyed hereafter by you.

I am sir your hble servant,

JNO. TODD.

15th June 1779.

I recommend 4 or 5 from your Compy and as many from Capt. Placey and consult Mr. Lacroix about the time necessary.

J. T."

Nicholas Janis was, as we have seen, Captain of the first Company of Militia at Kaskaskia, and the Captain Placey mentioned is, undoubtedly, Joseph Duplessis, Captain of the second Company at the same place.   Kohos. was the familiar abbreviation of Cahokia, and the Mr. Le Croix, who was to be consulted, must have been J. B. L. Croix, first sheriff of the Cahokia district, by whom, no doubt, the execution of Moreau was conducted.   These two entries, therefore, confirm Reynold's account of this matter, the accuracy of which has sometimes been questioned, and give to old Cahokia the sad distinction of having been a Western Salem.

The different subjects thus far included in this interesting Record-Book, were all dealt with by Todd between May 14th and June 15th, 1779.   He certainly was not idle, nor did he lack for important business during the first month of his administration.   His duties appear then to have called him away from Kaskaskia, probably to Vincennes, to make the appointments there already noticed.   And as he was about to leave, he addressed a letter to his deputy-commandant, Richard Winston, which is sufficiently interesting to be quoted entire.

"Sir: During my absence the command will devolve upon you as commander of Kaskaskia.—if Colo. Clark should want anything more for his expedition, consult the members of the court upon the best mode of proceeding, if the people will not spare wilingly, if in their power, you must press it, valuing the property by Two men upon Oath.—let the military have no pretext for forcing property—When you order it and the people will not find it, then it will be Time for them to Interfere.—by all means Keep up a Good Understanding with Colo. Clark and the Officers.—if this is not the Case you will be unhappy.   I am sir

Yr Hble Servt JOHN TODD

June 15, 1779."

The expedition of Colonel Clark, referred to in this letter, is supposed to have been that planned against the British at Detroit, which he and Governor Henry were very anxious to undertake.   They were ultimately prevented by lack of means. Todd's determination to keep the military in subordination to the civil power is very plain, but at the same time his doubt of his success, and his appreciation of Clark's peculiarities, are curiously shown by the concluding paragraph of this letter. When he tells Richard Winston by all means to keep up a good understanding with Colo. Clark, and that, if this is not the case, he will be unhappy, he evidently is speaking of that of which he knows by personal experience.

Upon his return to Kaskaskia, July 27th, 1779, the resolutions of Congress concerning the issues of the continental money, dated May 20th, 1777, and April 11th, 1778, engaged his attention. And he put forth a short proclamation in French and English, both copies being duly transcribed in his Record at pages 19 and 20, notifying persons having money of those issues that unless they shall as soon as possible pay the same into some continental treasury, the money must sink on their hands, and that the vouchers must be certified by himself or some deputy-commandant of this county, and have reference to the bundle of money numbered and sealed. Whether this Congressional plan superceded that of Todd's own devising, we do not know, but at all events we hear nothing further of his land fund.

It would appear that during his brief absence, the newly-appointed court at Kaskaskia had not transacted business with the diligence and celerity required by John Todd. The judges were all elected from among the French settlers, and we may assume that their easy-going ways did not find favor with the busy man from beyond the Ohio. They seem to have adjourned court to what appeared to him to be too long a day, and his consequent action savors somewhat of a direct interference of the executive with the judiciary, but, doubtless, was effective. On page 21 we read the following document:

"To Gabriel Cerre &c. Esqrs. Judges of the Court for the District of Kaskaskia:

You are hereby authorized and required to hold and constitute a court on Satterday, the 21st of July at the usual place of holding court within yr District, any adjournment to the contrary notwithstanding. Provided that no suitor or party be compeled to answear any process upon said Day unless properly summoned by the Clark and Sheriff. Given under my hand and seal at Kaskaskia July 31st 1779. JOHN TODD."

He was tender of the rights of parties, but proposed that the judges should attend to their work. Doubtless, Gabriel and his associates grumbled not a little at this interference with their comfort, and insisted, the one to the other, that they had not accepted the judicial office upon any such understanding. Pleasure first and business afterwards, had always been the rule at Kaskaskia, and to compel a man to hold court when he preferred to smoke his pipe in the' sun, or go fishing, was an unprecedented hardship. But all the same, we may be very sure that they did "hold and constitute a court on Satterday the 21st of July, any adjournment to the contrary notwithstanding."

Mindful of Governor Henry's advice to cultivate a connection with the Spanish commandant, near Kaskaskia, Commandant

Todd sends a letter, in French, on August 9th, 1779, to Monsieur Cartabonne, commanding at St. Genevieve, and a letter to same effect to Monsieur Leyba, at St. Louis. It will be remembered that all the region west of the Mississippi then belonged to Spain, at that time at war with Britian, and was garrisoned by her troops. In these letters he proposes an arrangement concerning the commerce of the Illinois country, for the mutual advantage of their respective governments, his Catholic Majesty on the one hand, and the State of Virginia on the other, and for the disadvantage of their common enemy, the British. He informs the Spaniards that Colonel Clark has not yet departed from Post Vincennes, and further states that, if they are attacked by any enemies, and he can be of service to them, he is ordered by the Governor of Virginia to give aid to them.

The slow-moving French settlers seem to have been in other ways a trial, and probably were dilatory in providing supplies for the troops, which were soon expected from Virginia. And on Aug. 11th, Todd enters, on page 22 of his Book, a brief address, in which the inhabitants of Kaskaskia are, for the last time, invited to contract with the persons appointed for provision, especially "Flower," for the troops who will shortly arrive. He says, "I hope they will use properly the Indulgence of a mild Government. If I shall be obliged to give the military permission to press It will be a disadvantage, and what ought more to influence Freemen, it will be a dishonor to the people." It is evident that Baptiste, Francois, and the rest, while willing enough to be "Freemen," on their money still preferred a king. And the supplies which they would have readily furnished in exchange for coins stamped with the head of George III. or Louis XV., were not forthcoming when continental currency was offered in return, despite all of Todd's efforts in that behalf. It is said that the early French inhabitants were so puzzled by the machinery of free government, that they longed for the return of the despotic authority of their military commandants. If so, there must have been a familiar sound about this brief address which might have made them think their good old times had come again. After this he copies an order upon the Governor of Virginia, in favor of J. B. La Croix, the Sheriff of Cahokia, in payment of supplies furnished, probably one of the few, if not the only one who paid any attention to the address.

The Commandant found it necessary to resort to more stringent measures. And on August 22d, he issued another proclamation laying an embargo upon the exportation of any provisions whatsoever, by land or water, for sixty days, unless he has

assurances before that time that a sufficient stock is laid up for
the troops, or sufficient security is given to the contractors for its
delivery when required.   And the offender is to be subjected to
imprisonment for one month and forfeit value of such exported
provision.   This he records in English and in French, apparently
having special reference to those of the latter race.   And seemingly becoming weary of the delay of the people as to the
surrender of the continental money, he gives notice, in both
languages, that after August 23d, 1779, no more certificates will
be granted at Kaskaskia to persons producing the called-in
emissions.   It does not appear whether this delay was due to the
fact that the prudent French settlers really had no continental
money on hand, or to their wish to get some return for what
little they did own, and they were unable to see any such outcome
from a deposit in a continental treasury.

October 7th, 1779, he makes a note of an order given to
Patrick M'Crosky on the Gov't for 140 Dollars being No. 2
issued "by a certificate from Mr. Helm."   This Mr. Helm was
one of Clark's trusty lieutenants, and was, probably, then commanding the fort at Vincennes.

A short and simple method of forfeiting realty to the State, is
illustrated in the proceedings set forth on pages 25 and 26.   On
the 4th of October, 1779, a notification was given at the door of
the church of Kaskaskia, that the half-a-lot above the church,
joining Picard on the east, and Langlois on the west, unless some
person should appear and support their claim to the said lot
within three days, would be condemned to the use of the Commonwealth.   On the 13th day of October, 1779, accordingly,
John Todd, under his hand and seal, at Kaskaskia, proclaimed
that after publicly calling any person or persons to shew any
claim they might have to said lot, and no one appearing to
claim the same as against the Commonwealth of Virginia, he
declares and adjudges the said lot to belong to the said Commonwealth, and that all persons, whatsoever, be thenceforth
debarred and precluded forever from any claim thereto.

The heading of the following entry in this book is, "Copy of
a Grant to Colonel Montgomery," but the remainder of that
page, and one or two more, have been deliberately torn out.
The explanation of this mutilation may be found in a report
made, in 1810, by the Commissioners appointed by Congress to
examine the claims of persons claiming lands in the district of
Kaskaskia, from which it appears that many of the ancient
evidences of title had been deliberately destroyed in the interest
of speculators claiming under forged deeds or perjured testimony.

Some one, interested in opposition to this grant, may have had access to this book years after the entry, when the land had become valuable, and attempted to defeat the title in this way. The Colonel Montgomery, named in it, was probably the Captain Montgomery who came to the Illinois with Clark, and rendered good service on that expedition. He is described as a jovial Irishman, whom Clark fell in with at the Falls of the Ohio, on his way down the river, and who readily joined in the perilous adventure, from pure love of fighting. He commanded the garrison of Fort Gage, at Kaskaskia, after its surrender by the British.

This is the last entry in the book in Todd's handwriting.

We know that he continued to hold his position as Commandant and County-Lieutenant at the Illinois for some three years more, devoting most of his time to its affairs. And in that period he made the difficult and often dangerous journey between his distant post and the Kentucky settlements, or Virginia, two or more times in every year. In 1779, Virginia ordered two regiments to be raised for service in its western counties, and it is supposed that Todd was appointed Colonel of one of them. In the spring of 1780, he was elected a delegate from the county of Kentucky to the Legislature of Virginia, and was married while attending its session of that year. In the fall, he returned to Kentucky, and, having established his bride in the fort at Lexington, resumed his journey to Illinois. It is worthy of remark that the foundation of Transylvania University, the first institution of learning west of the mountains, is attributed to the State aid obtained from the Virginia Legislature by his exertions in its behalf. In November, 1780, the county of Kentucky was divided into the three counties of Fayette, Lincoln, and Jefferson, and in the summer of 1781, Governor Thomas Jefferson appointed Todd, Colonel of Fayette County, Daniel Boone, Lieutenant-Colonel, and Thomas Marshall, (father of Chief-Justice Marshall), Surveyor. In December, 1781, Todd secured a town lot at Lexington, and in May, 1782, he was made one of the trustees of Lexington by Act of Virginia. In the summer of that year he visited Richmond, on the business of the Illinois country, where it is said he had concluded to permanently reside, and stopped at Lexington on his return. While here, an Indian attack upon a frontier station summoned the militia to arms, and he, as Senior Colonel, took command of the little force of 180 men who went in pursuit of the retreating savages. It included Daniel Boone and many other pioneers of note, sixty of their number being commissioned officers. At the Blue Licks, on the

18th of August, 1782, the enemy was overtaken, and the head-long courage of those who would not observe the prudent counsels of Todd and Boone, precipitated an action which was very disastrous to the whites. One-third of those who went into battle were killed, a number wounded and several made prisoners. And among the heroes who laid down their lives that day was Colonel John Todd. He was shot through the body while gallantly fighting at the head of his men, and, says an eye-witness, "When last seen he was reeling in his saddle, while the blood gushed in profusion from his wounds."

A few other minutes were made in this book in Colonel Todd's life-time, which are not in his handwriting. On two pages, near the end, is kept his "Peltry Account," which is charged with his drafts on the Virginia Government, in favor of Monsieur Beauregarde, to the amount of $30,000, dated at St. Louis, September 14th, 1779, the value thereof having, apparently, been received, one-third in paper currency and two-thirds in peltries. The account is credited with payments made for supplies for the garrison at Kaskaskia, purchased by Colonel John Montgomery, and for the garrison at Cahokia, purchased by Capt. M'Carthy, probably that Richard M'Carthy, gentleman, to whom a "License for Trade" was granted, as we have seen. The principal item in these supplies seems to have been a beverage called "Taffia," which was laid in by the hogshead. On page 28 is an oath of allegiance taken by one James Moore, at Kaskaskia, to the United States of America, on July 10th, 1872, while the States were still under the articles of confederation, showing the form then used. He renounces all fidelity to King George the Third, King of Great Britain, his heirs and successors, and agrees to make known to some one Justice of the Peace for the United States, all treasonous, all traitorous conspiracies which may come to his knowledge to be formed against said United States, or any one of them.

During Todd's later absences from his government, a French gentleman named Demunbrunt, appears to have been his deputy and acting-commandant in his place. And it is curious to notice on the inside of one of the covers of this book a little penmanship, which may indicate that this individual was rather proud of his temporary dignity. It reads "Nota bene, Nous Thimothé Demunbrunt Lt. Comdt Par interim &c &c;" and it seems as if Thimothé could not resist the temptation to see how his name and title would look, and so wrote it out in a fine, bold hand for all men to see for a hundred years to come. On the last page are two memoranda, apparently in the same bold hand, which, in pencil underneath, are said to be by Thimothé Demunbrunt Lt. Comdt par interim, and, doubless, this is correct. They read: "February 1782, Arived a small tribe of the Wabash Indians Imploring the paternal succour of their Father the Bostonians, having their patent from Major Linctot, in consequence I did on Behalf of the Commonwealth give them Six Bushell Indian Corn, Fifty Pounds of Bread, four Pounds of Gun Powder, Ten Pounds of Ball and One Gallon of Taffia, from Carbonneaux." And, "March 22d, Came here Deputys from the Delawars, Shawanoes and Cherokee nations of Indians Begging that the Americans wold grant them Pease, as likewise the French and Spanish, and after hearing their Talk, Smoaking the pipe of peace and friendship with them, and from their conduct while here as well as many marks they gave us of their Sincerity I could not avoid giving them on Behalf of the Americans the Following articles, vizt.

10 Bushells Indian Corn, 100 lb. Flour and 100 lb. Bisquit, 6 lb. Tobaco, one Gallon Tafia, 5 qts wampum and Canoe which cost me 20 Dollars."

The use of the word "Bostonians" by the Wabash Indians, to indicate the whites, is interesting, and may, perhaps, show that this tribe contained or was made up of fragments of tribes of New England Indians, who would naturally use this phrase. The evidence furnished by these memoranda of the weakness and destitution of once powerful Indian nations, is very striking, although their real condition may have been slightly exaggerated, in order to obtain larger supplies of Tafia. Probably they fared better at the hands of the simple Frenchman, from the good-will of his race to the red man, than if Colonel Todd had been at the helm.

But, it may be asked, what had become of Richard Winston, who was Deputy-Commandant in the early part of Todd's administration, and how came he to be superseded by this softhearted Thimothé?

We should have been utterly unable to answer these questions but for a paragraph written upon the inside of the front cover of this book, which is as follows:

"Kaskaskias in the Illinois 29th April 1782. This day 10 o'clock A.M. I was taken out of my house by J. Neal Dodge on an order given by Jno. Dodge in despite of the Civil authority disregarding the laws, and on the malitious alugation of Jno. Williams and Michel Pevante as may appear by their deposition. I was confined by tyrannick military force without making any legal aplication to the Civil Magistrates—30th The Attorney for the

State, La Buinieux, presented a petition to the court against Richard Winston, State Prisoner in their custody the contents of which he (the Attorney for the State) ought to have communicated to me or my attorney, if any I had." It will be remembered that when Todd first went away from Kaskaskia, leaving Winston in command, he advised him, by letter, by all means to keep up a good understanding with Colonel Clark and the officers, telling him if this was not the case he would be unhappy. We can only conclude that the unlucky Winston had at this time neglected this injunction, as his trouble seems to have been with the military, and in consequence was very unhappy. At all events he had fallen into disgrace, of course had lost his office, and was imprisoned, doubtless, in the old French commandant's house, which served as the headquarters of the successive governments of the Illinois country, even down to the organization of our State when it became the first State House. Here shut up, perhaps in the governor's room, he found this Record-Book, and wrote his sorrowful tale within it. And so it preserves to us, a century after, poor Richard Winston's protest against "tyrannick military force."

The remaining pages of this book are occupied with a brief record in the French language of the proceedings of the Court of Kaskaskia, from June 5th, 1787, to February 15th, 1788. During this period it seems to be pretty much in the hands of one family, as three of the five justices are named Beauvais. Antoine Beauvais is the presiding justice, and Vital Beauvais, and St. Gemme Beauvais, are two of his four associates. For a long time they apparently do nothing but meet one month and adjourn to the next, as if determined in this way to regain the dignity of which the court was deprived by Col. Todd's peremptory order to their predecessors to hold a session, despite their order of adjournment. On October 25th, 1787, they settle down to business, at what they call an extraordinary session, to try a case between our good friend Demunbrunt, and one Francis Carboneaux. It will be remembered that Thimothé bought the Tafia he gave to the Indians from Carboneaux, and perhaps he had forgotten to pay for it. The details, and the result of the cause, are not given. The court pursues the even tenor of its way with commendable regularity, meeting once a month, in the morning, and immediately adjourning to the next month, but holding an extraordinary session whenever it had a case to try, (and it had two, all told), until January 15th, 1788. At this date, it, for the first time, seemingly, has to deal with the subject of jurymen, and solemnly determines that each juror from Prairie du Rocher shall have twenty-five francs, and thereupon adjourns. It meets in the afternoon and impanels a jury to try a cause in which John Edgar is plaintiff, and Thomas Green, defendant, and with a few similar minutes its record ceases, and this book comes to an end.

Its own story is curious enough to entitle it to preservation, if only for its age and the vicissitudes through which it has passed. Made in Virginia more than one hundred years ago, brought the long journey thence to Illinois, at that day exceeding in risk and time a modern trip around the world, in use here in the infancy of the Republic, then cast aside and forgotten for almost a century, and lately rescued by the merest chance from destruction, it has now, by the formal vote of the Board of Commissioners of Randolph County, Illinois, the lineal successors of our first County-Lieutenant, been placed, we hope permanently, in the custody of the Chicago Historical Society. And when we consider that its opening pages were inscribed by the first Governor of the State of Virginia, who was one of the foremost men of the Revolution, that it is mainly filled with the handiwork of the first County-Lieutenant of the great North-West Territory, that it contains the record of one of the first courts of common law in Illinois, and above all, that it is a summary of the beginning of Republican institutions here, and, in fact, the record of the origin of our State, this common-looking book, with its coarse paper and few pages of faded handwriting, becomes an unique historical memorial, worthy to be treasured by the people of Illinois with reverent care for all time to come.

And with it too should be treasured the memory of that brave and able man, John Todd, a pioneer of progress, education, and liberty, and the real founder of this Commonwealth, who served his countrymen long and well, and died a noble death, fighting for their homes and firesides against a savage enemy, and giving his life, as he had given the best of his years and strength, for the cause of civilization and free government in the Western World.

The foregoing Paper was read before the Chicago Historical Society, Feb. 15, 1881.

THE MARTYRDOM OF LOVEJOY.

account of the Life, Trials, and Perils of Rev. Elijah P. Lovejoy, killed by
Slavery Mob, at Alton, Ill., on the night of Nov. 7, 1637. By HENRY TANNER, of Buffalo, N.Y., a
Witness. Cloth boards; Gilt-top; Side and bottom uncut; Illustrated; Pp. 233; 8vo.   1881.   Pri

An exceedingly interesting and fully authentic narrative of one of the most thrilling episodes in the history of the great anti-slavery movement which culminated in the War of the Rebellion and the emancipation of the slaves by President Lincoln. But for such books as this, it would be difficult for us, in this day, to realize what heroic courage, what patience in suffering and self-sacrifice it required to stand up against the bitter opposition which the publication of anti-slavery sentiments elicited in the dark days of 1837, when Lovejoy published the Alton *Observer*. There is no doubt but that Lovejoy's name will go into history as the first American martyr for the right of free speech and a free press. He was a brave, great-souled, clear-headed man, and, like Samson of old, it may be said of him that he slew more Philistines at his death than in all his life. The publishers of this and other valuable documents relating to the early history of our State, are doing a good work for the general public and for posterity. They rank among the oldest printing companies of the City, and it seems peculiarly appropriate that they should seek to rescue from fast-approaching oblivion all accessible facts relating to early pioneer life within the bounds of our glorious Commonwealth. The "Martyrdom of Lovejoy" is not the only valuable work which has already issued from their press, and which they keep constantly on hand for sale.—*Chicago Journal*, Feb. 5, 1881.

The story is deeply interesting, and now seems almost incredible, so far have we risen beyond the stagnant condition in which Lovejoy's death found us. The book is handsomely printed and contains a few engravings and fac-similes,—one, a head of Lovejoy himself, who does not look like a great man, but like a good one, as in fact he was,—brave and earnest and well fitted to be a martyr.—*Springfield Republi'n*, Mass., March 24th, 1881.

Not only to those who at the time were personally interested in the career and heroic death of the Rev. Elijah Parrish Lovejoy, nor to those who now warmly sympathize with the noble purposes which prompted the martyr to the pursuit of ends apparently chimerical in the extent of their nobility; but to all students of the germs and first budding of a mighty reformation in the history of morals, and to all lovers of mysterious natural development this book will be valuable. Here is vividly portrayed the first blood-letting for outspoken antagonism to the villainies of slave-traffic and slave-holding, and the wonderful persistence in aim, as well as the power of thought and pen that prepared Lovejoy for his glorious end. From the early articles on transubstantiation and nunneries to the last fiery denunciation of negro subjection, the hero shows the same outspoken boldness of conviction, combined with a continual increase in ability of expression. That any pledge was violated in the assumption of an anti-slavery

tone in the leaders of the *St. Louis Obs*
Mr. Tanner has clearly proved groundless
that the life of Elijah Parrish Lovejoy is w
to be ranked among the highest and pure
candid reader can pretend to doubt. "So a
a good deed in a naughty world."—*Buffal
press*, May 18, 1881.

Probably no single event in the early h
of the progress of the anti-slavery sentim
the United States, produced a more pro
impression at the time than the successi

civil authority, he sacrificed his life. These
annals of the anti-slavery agitation can w
perused by many who lived at the time,
to the student of American history, wh
been born since those years, they are in
ble.—*Iowa State Register*, May 14, 1881.

The "Martyrdom of Lovejoy" is the titl
well-printed octavo volume, published b
Fergus Printing Company, of Chicago,
contains an account of the life, trials, and
of Rev. Elijah P. Lovejoy. * * * The a
Henry Tanner, of Buffalo, N. Y., who as
Mr. Lovejoy in the defence of his propert
his rights, and was by his side when he
has done a valuable service in gathering,
the records of the past, so many items o
toric interest to combine with his own rec
tions of the tragic event which shook the
country like an earthquake.—*Sunday H
Boston*, March 6, 1881.

This is a plain, unvarnished history o
life and perils of the Rev. Elijah P. Lo
* * * So rapid has been the march of
sentiment that the generation of young me

deadly antagonism of slavery forty-three
ago. The book will give an insight into th
ter and unrelenting spirit which held swa
in the free North. It is not written to

all that has been accomplished in the pas
appreciate the present. The story is told
out any effort at embellishment, and wo
fully free from every vindictive expressio
the friends of human slavery object to an
in the volume, it will be the honest facts
history, which need no embellishment or
phrase to make them abhorrent to every
of the right and free institutions.—*Inter O
Chicago*, Feb. 5, 1881.

As the narrative has reference to events
since past, connected with the early days
anti-slavery contest, we had no idea unt
began reading the book that we should fi
so deeply interesting and well calculated t
an insight into the struggle for the libe
the press which led to the abolition of sl
—*Messiah's Herald*, Boston, March 30, 18

Reception to the Settlers of Chicago, prior to 1840, by the CALUMET CLUB, Ma
1879. Containing Club Members' Names; Origin of Reception; Record of Old Settlers invited; Rec
Speeches of Rev. Stephen R. Beggs, Gen Henry Strong, Ex.-Chief-Justice John Dean Caton, Judge
W. Blodgett, Judge James Grant, Hon. John Wentworth, Judge Grant Goodrich, Hon. J. Young Sca
and Hon. Wm. Bross; Tables showing places of birth, year of arrival, and age of those who attende
signed Register; Appendix with letters from John Watkins, Norman K. Towner. Rev. Flavel Bascom,
Gen. David Hunter, Judge Ebenezer Peck. Rev. Jeremiah Porter, and the names from whom brief
of regret were received; Extracts from *Chicago Tribune* and *Evening Journal*; and Register
Settlers; with name, date of arrival, birthplace, age, and present address. Compiled by Hon.
WENTWORTH. Pp 90; 8vo. 1879.   Price, 50

Sent by mail, post-paid, on receipt of price.

FERGUS' HISTORICAL SERIE

1.

Annals of Chicago: A Lecture read before the Chicago Lyceum, Jan. 21, 1840. By JOSEPH N. BALESTIER, Esq., Republished from the original edition of 1840, with an Introduction, written by the Author in 1876; and, also, a Review of the Lecture, published in the *Chicago Tribune*, in 1872. Pp. 48; 8vo. 1876. Price, 25 cents.

2.

Fergus' Directory of the City of Chicago, 1839; with City and County Officers, Churches, Public Buildings, Hotels, etc.; also, list of Sheriffs of Cook County and Mayors of the City since their organization; together with the Poll-list of the First City Election (Tuesday, May 2, 1837). List of Purchasers of Lots in Fort-Dearborn Addition, the No. of the Lots and the prices paid, etc., etc. (Historical Sketch of City compiled for Directory of 1843, etc.) Compiled by ROBERT FERGUS. Pp. 68; 8vo. 1876. Price, 50 cents.

3.

The Last of the Illinois, and a Sketch of the Pottawatomies: A Lecture read before the Chicago Historical Society, Dec. 13, 1870. Also, **Origin of the Prairies:** A Lecture read before the Ottawa Academy of Natural Sciences, Dec. 30, 1869. By Hon. JOHN DEAN CATON, LL.D., late Chief-Justice of Illinois. Pp. 56; 8vo. 1876. Price, 25 cts.

4.

Early Movement in Illinois for the Legalization of Slavery: An Historical Sketch read at the Annual Meeting of the Chicago Historical Society, Dec. 5, 1864. By Hon. WM. H. BROWN. Pp. 32; 8vo. 1876. Price, 25 cents.

5.

Biographical Sketches of Early Settlers of Chicago—Part I.—Hon. S. Lisle Smith, Geo. Davis, Dr. Phillip Maxwell, John J. Brown, Richard L. Wilson, Col. Lewis C. Kerchival, Uriah P. Harris, Henry B. Clarke, and Sheriff Samuel J. Lowe. By W. H. BUSHNELL. Pp. 48; 8vo. 1876. Price, 25 cts.

6.

Biographical Sketches of Early Settlers of Chicago. Part II.—Hon. Wm. H. Brown, with ... , B. W. Raymond, Esq., with Portrait, Hon. ... mmon, Chas. Walker, Esq., Thos. Church, ... 48; 8vo. 1876. Price, 25 cents.

7.

Early Chicago: A Sunday Lecture read in McCormick's Hall, May 7th, 1876. With Supplemental Notes. 2d Lecture. By Hon. JOHN WENTWORTH. Portrait. Pp. 56; 8vo. 1876. Price, 35 cts.

8.

Early Chicago: A Sunday Lecture read in McCormick's Hall, April 11, 1875. With Supplemental Notes. 1st Lecture. By Hon. JOHN WENTWORTH. Portrait. Pp. 48; 8vo. 1876. Price, 35 cts.

9.

Present and Future Prospects of Chicago: An Address read before the Chicago Lyceum, Jan. 20, 1846. By Judge HENRY BROWN, author of "History of Illinois."
Rise and Progress of Chicago: An Address read before the Centennial Library Association, March 21, 1876. By JAMES A. MARSHALL, Esq.
Chicago in 1836: "Strange Early Days." By HARRIET MARTINEAU, author of "Society in America," etc. Pp. 48; 8vo. 1876. Price, 25 cents.

10.

Addresses Read before Chicago Historical Society, By Hon J. Y. SCAMMON, Hon. I. N. ARNOLD, WM. HICKLING, Esq., Col. G. S HUBBARD, and HIRAM W. BECKWITH, Esq.; Sketches of Col. John H. Kinzie, by his wife, JULIETTE A. KINZIE; Judge Geo. Manierre, Luther Haven, Esq.,

and other Early Settlers; also, of Billy Cal Shabonee, and the "Winnebago Scare," of J and other important original matter conne " Early Chicago." Pp. 52; 8vo. 1877.

11.

Early Medical Chicago: An His Sketch of the First Practitioners of Medi the Present Faculties, and Graduates since ganization of the Medical Colleges of Chi JAMES NEVINS HYDE, A.M., M.D. Illust numerous Wood Engravings and Steel Engr Professors J. Adams Allen, N. S. Davis, an Daniel Brainard. Pp. 84; 8vo. 1879. Pric

12.

Illinois in the 18th Century.—Ka and its Parish Records. A Paper rea the Chicago Historical Society, Dec. 16, 1
Old Fort Chartres: A Paper read before cago Historical Society, June 16, 1880. gram of Fort.
Col. John Todd's Record Book. A Pa before the Chicago Historical Society, Feb. By EDWARD G. MASON. Pp. 68; 8vo. 1881

13.

Recollections of Early Illinois a Noted Men. By Hon. JOSEPH GILLES wardsville. Read before the Chicago Society, March 16, 1880 With Portraits o Govs. Reynolds and Bissell, and Henry Pp. 52; 8vo. 1880. Price,

14.

The Earliest Religious History of C By Rev. JEREMIAH PORTER. its 1st Residen An Address read before the Chicago Hist.
Early History of Illinois. By Hon. WIL BROWN. A Lecture read before the Chi ceum, Dec. 8, 1840.
Early Society in Southern Illinois. ROBERT W. PATTERSON, D.D. An Addr before the Chicago Historical Society, Oct.
Reminiscences of the Illinois-Bar Fort Ago: Lincoln and Douglas as Orators and By Hon. ISAAC N. ARNOLD. Read before t Bar Association, Springfield, Jan 7, 1881.
The First Murder-Trial in Iroquois Cou the First Murder in Cook County. Pp. 1 1881 Price, 5

15.

Abraham Lincoln: A Paper read bef Royal Historical Society, London, June 1 By Hon. ISAAC N. ARNOLD, of Chicago.
Stephen Arnold Douglas, An Eulogy. ed before the Chicago University, in Brya July 3, 1861. By Hon JAMES W. SHEA *The Chicago Tribune.* 1881. 8vo., 48 pp. Price, 2

16.

Early Chicago—Fort Dearborn: A dress read at the unveiling of a tablet on t site, under the auspices of the Chicago H Society, Chicago, May 21, 1881. 3d Pa Hon. JOHN WENTWORTH, LL.D. With an dix, etc., etc. Portraits of Capt. Wm. Wells Capt. Heald. Also, Indexes to 1st and 2d and "Calumet-Club Reception." 8vo., 112

17.

Wm. B. Ogden; and Early Days cago. By Hon. ISAAC N. ARNOLD. (In

18.

Chicago River-and-Harbor Conve Held July 5th, 1847. (In

19.

Reminiscences of Early Chicago. CHARLES CLEAVER. (In